MW01007237

The Serpent's Skin

MARC KLEIN

The Serpent's Skin

Creation, Knowledge, and Intimacy in the Book of Genesis

URIM PUBLICATIONS
Jerusalem ◆ New York

The Serpent's Skin: Creation, Knowledge, and Intimacy
in the Book of Genesis
by Marc Klein

ISBN 13: 978-965-524-054-2
Printed in Israel
First Edition

Book design by Ariel Walden

Urim Publications
P.O. Box 52287, Jerusalem 91521, Israel

Lambda Publishers Inc.
527 Empire Blvd., Brooklyn, New York 11225, USA
Tel: 718-972-5449   Fax: 718-972-6307
mh@ejudaica.com

www.UrimPublications.com

Contents

Preface

IN THE COURSE OF READING AND REREADING GENESIS over the years it struck me how it would often happen that I would notice something—an odd expression, a group of similar-sounding words, the use of a particular kind of imagery—that seemed to be hinting at some idea or some relation between one text and another, but it would not be immediately obvious what this idea or connection might be. Often these intriguing glimmers led to a dead end, but sometimes they would result in a fuller understanding of a story, and at the same time, a better grasp of some of the techniques that undergird the narratives. For example, in the story of Jacob, Jacob's elder brother Esau is nicknamed Edom because he is ruddy at birth and because at one point he sells his birthright to Jacob for some red stew, and the Hebrew for "red" is ADoM—which has the same consonants as Edom (see page 21 for transliteration of Hebrew into English). Edom is the name of the nation that is said to be descended from Esau. When Jacob flees his brother's anger he finds refuge with their uncle, whose name is Laban. Laban means "white." There appears to be some kind of play with color imagery here, but what—if anything—does it mean?

Once the story is understood as a morality tale with a certain point of view, the significance of the colors becomes clear (see Chapter 6). My grounds for reading the story in this way are completely independent of the color imagery, but the juxtaposition of the two colors has the effect of lending further support to this particular reading.

As a second example, take the genealogical listing of the generations from Adam, the first man, to Noah, the survivor of the great Flood (Genesis 5:1–31). There are many other genealogical lists in Genesis, but this one is unique in that each short biographical notice ends with the phrase "and he died." No other list has this feature. In every other list we are told that so-and-so lived X number of years, and then that his son lived Y number of years, and so on. Why was it important to tell us that each of the men of the generations from Adam to Noah died (with one exception)?

An explanation for these repeated death announcements suggests itself once the story of Noah is understood to have reference to the original account of the Creation, and especially to the story of Adam and Eve in the Garden of Eden (see Chapter 4). Needless to say, the explanation that I propose is just that—a suggestion. There may be other explanations, but what I have come up with has the advantage of also fitting into a larger view of what the narratives have to say.

The pleasure of discovering within the texts interrelations that were not evident on a first reading, together with the satisfaction of understanding the unique ways that these interrelations are forged, led me to continue reading and rereading Genesis attentively, with an open mind. How this way of looking at the Book of Genesis sheds light on the meaning of the narratives is something that I would like to share with other readers.

◆ ◎ ◆

The Book of Genesis is made up of two parts. The first part covers the first eleven chapters of the book and deals with the primeval history of the world and of humanity. This history comprises the stories of the Creation, the Garden of Eden, the Flood, the Tower of Babel, and a number of genealogical lists and other material. The second part is the patriarchal history, which tells of the beginnings of the Hebrew nation, or the Children of Israel. The patriarchal history begins with the story of Abraham and continues through the stories of the first few generations of Abraham's progeny until the death of his great-grandson Joseph.

The primeval history is presented in relatively short and self-contained narratives that contain little in the way of real characters or character development, while the stories of the patriarchal history show a progressive elaboration and deepening in the portrayal of the protagonists and their interactions. The schematic nature of the narratives in the primeval history allows for more interpretative freedom, and my reading of these stories will be correspondingly looser and more speculative. By contrast, the fuller treatment of the Patriarchs in the later portions of Genesis puts more in the way of constraints on how these narratives can be read, as we will see. I have therefore divided my book into two parts to reflect these differences.

Part One, consisting of the three chapters following the Introduction, deals with motifs of creation and introduces the contrasting perspectives of God and humans. Outlines of the irreducible characteristics of humanity are also drawn here. These universal themes form a context for the stories of the patriarchal history that are discussed in Part Two. Although many of the literary techniques that I discuss below are used throughout Genesis, they are exploited most fully in the stories of the Patriarchs.

In the Epilogue, I show how some of the motifs that were introduced in the stories of the Creation are carried over into the second book of the Pentateuch, the Book of Exodus, and from there into the Book of Joshua.

◆ ◎ ◆

This book presents an interpretation of the Book of Genesis that treats it as an interconnected whole, as opposed to a collection of independent, unrelated stories. Looking at the book as a whole allows us to see connections within and between narratives that might not be obvious otherwise, and these connections often suggest a particular understanding of one or another episode or narrative cycle. In particular, looking at the text in this way sometimes reveals a point of view—not necessarily expressed explicitly—that the text takes with respect to the personalities and actions of the protagonists.

By no means am I implying that the text is a seamless and orderly narrative in which everything has its place in relation to everything else—far from it. There are many parts of the book that are not related in any obvious way to any other part, and it would not be useful to try to force everything into a single framework. Nevertheless, examining the relations among different parts of the book often helps to clarify what the stories are actually saying. What I understand to be the significance of these interconnections will be persuasive to varying degrees, and some of my interpretations will necessarily be no more than tentative suggestions. I leave it to the reader to evaluate the persuasiveness of any particular suggestion of mine.

◆ ◎ ◆

First, some historical perspective. There have been, broadly speaking, three approaches to interpreting the Jewish Bible over the past two and a half millennia. The most ancient is a genre generally termed "Midrash," which involves extracting meanings—not necessarily apparent on the surface—by close analysis of the text, especially by paying attention to verbal clues that point to the hidden messages. These interpretations tend to be homiletical and tendentious, and very often stray quite far from what appears to be the plain sense of the text in order not to violate the assumptions that underlie this kind of reading. The major guiding assumptions of these interpreters are explained by James L. Kugel in two of his books.[1]

One common assumption of classical Midrash, for example, is that when a character who is deemed to be irreproachable in his behavior—as is presumed to be true of the Patriarchs above all—commits what looks like an immoral or a questionable act, the narrative must be interpreted in such a way as to make this act not be what it appears to be. An illustration of this procedure is found in the treatment of the story of Jacob in the Book of Genesis. In the course of tricking his blind father, Isaac, into bestowing on him the blessing meant for his elder brother, Jacob lies to his father. Isaac asks, "Who are you, my son?" and Jacob responds, "I am Esau, your firstborn son." An ancient reading of this conversation turns Jacob's response on its head by inserting a pause into his answer without actually changing the words of the original Hebrew: "It is I; Esau is your firstborn son." The story then turns into something completely different from what a casual reader might have thought. Jacob does not really lie, and Isaac's bestowing the blessing on him is actually the realization of a divine plan. Jacob, Isaac, Esau, and the other protagonists of the story are treated as real people whose actions are motivated by their individual perceptions, desires, and judgments—but these may not be what they appear to be on the surface.

The most recent approach to reading the Hebrew Bible, in some ways the polar opposite of Midrash, is that taken by Bible scholars of the last two centuries or so.² These scholars rely on any and all relevant material unearthed by archaeology, on newly discovered texts from Near Eastern cultures contemporaneous with biblical periods, and, above all, on stylistic analysis of the biblical texts themselves that is thought to reveal the putative source documents from which the Bible was assembled. Modern Bible scholarship has availed itself of these tools to account for the inconsistencies and contradictions in the Bible as we have it. Scholars have proposed that inconsistencies arose when texts originating in different traditions or transmitted by different schools were incorporated side by side into the final version without a concerted effort by the compilers to reconcile the disagreements between the source texts.

More importantly, modern scholars have attempted to explain the significance of many biblical passages by seeking to identify the motives of the biblical authors or editors that prompted them to include a particular text. These explanations often result in a view of the biblical characters according to which they are no longer understood simply to be real individuals, but are rather representatives of national or political groups that played an important role at the time of the story's composition. The narratives are thus not morality tales about the actions and motives of real people, but rather stories that might represent the ascendancy or decline of this or that Israelite tribe, or this or that enemy nation. For example, the story of the struggle between the twin brothers Jacob and Esau for the birthright and blessing that we discussed briefly above is understood as reflecting the ascendancy in the tenth century BCE of the latecomer Israelite tribes over the established brother-nation of Edom, the other name of Esau.³

Interestingly, what these approaches—the Midrashic and the scholarly—have in common is that they both are not afraid to conclude that the text is not really saying what it appears to be saying. According to the Midrash, Jacob's lie is not really a lie, while according to some Bible scholars, Jacob is not really Jacob at all, but a personification of the Israelite nation of the tenth century BCE.

The third way of dealing with the texts of the Jewish Bible comprises approaches taken by the classical medieval Jewish commentators and their modern counterparts, as well as more purely literary treatments that have appeared in the past few decades.[4] Although these commentators differ from one another in some of their starting assumptions—even very fundamental ones, such as whether or not the text has a divine provenance, or whether the stories are history or fiction—and in the particular interpretative techniques they bring to bear, they all share the working assumption that the text means what it says, and they all try in one way or another to determine what that meaning is.

These interpreters all agree that the text as it stands should be respected as much as possible. So if the text recounts the actions of a man named Jacob, we should take these accounts at their face value, as being about a man named Jacob. In this respect, these interpreters agree with the approach of Midrash. The character Jacob may have special significance as a progenitor of the Israelite tribes and the later nation of Israel, but he is still portrayed as a human being whose actions in the stories about him are motivated by his wishes and intentions, which may in turn reflect traits in his personality. Any conclusions that we entertain should be based on what the text says, and not on any prior ideas that we might have about Jacob, or about how the text was put together. If the text has Jacob lying to his father, or taking advantage of his brother's weakness, it means what it says. We can try to understand Jacob's motives from how his story is told, and at the same time, we can try to discern whether the text portrays Jacob's actions in a negative, or positive, or neutral light—but still only on the basis of what the text tells us. And there is always the possibility that the text might give us no way of deciding one way or the other.

I will be taking the approach that what is important is what the text says, without relying on the assumptions accepted by either the Midrashic interpreters or the Bible scholars when these have no basis in the plain meaning of the text. This is certainly not a revolutionary approach, but is the way that innumerable commentators, both ancient and modern, have read the Bible. At the same time, however, I will rely on techniques reminiscent of those used by the authors of the ancient Midrashim. In particular, I will place great emphasis on the text's choice of particular words or expressions, whether in pointed word plays, or in the repetition of specific key words or roots, or in the use of odd or unique words where other, seemingly more suitable, words could have served just as easily. This way of reading can thus be considered to be a kind of Midrash.

My use of these tools differs from the way classical Midrash approaches the text in a number of ways. First, classical Midrash tends to be local, in the sense that a word or expression that appears in one place is linked to the same word or expression in a second place whether or not the broader contexts support a thematic connection. Classical Midrash also usually insists that the word or expression that appears in the two contexts be identical. By contrast, the connections that I will be discussing are more global in that they extend throughout a single story or between stories, and also may depend on word plays among similar roots rather than being limited to identical expressions. Perhaps most importantly, the verbal connections that we will be dealing with will be considered to be meaningful only if they are consonant with the inner logic of the stories, a criterion that is not taken into account in classical Midrash. In other words, there must be reasons for reading the narrative in a certain way that are independent of any single set of verbal connections alone.

These verbal techniques almost always depend on knowledge of the original Hebrew wording, which I will therefore provide in transliteration into Roman characters. I will describe these methods in detail in Chapter 1, "Frameworks," and will give a few examples here to give the reader an idea of how these techniques work. All the examples come from the story of Jacob.

The first example illustrates how the repeated use of a key word can shed light on the significance of the events in a narrative.

After a twenty-year separation from his elder brother, Esau, whose blessing he had appropriated by deceit, Jacob prepares to meet him by sending ahead a train of messengers with gifts for his brother. The text tells us what Jacob is thinking:

> For he reasoned, "If I propitiate him with presents in advance, and then face him, perhaps he will show me favor." And so the gift went on ahead, while he remained in the camp that night. (Genesis 32:21–22)[5]

This passage is followed by the famous story of Jacob's wrestling with an angel before he meets Esau. To commemorate his ordeal with the angel, Jacob names the place of the encounter Peniel (or Penuel), from the words for "face" and "divine being," for, as Jacob says, "I saw a divine being face to face and I survived" (32:31). Since the word for "divine being," Hebrew ELoHiM, is also used to refer to God, Peniel/ Penuel could equally well be translated as "the face of God."

At his meeting with Esau, which follows immediately afterward, Jacob insists that Esau accept his gifts and says:

> No, I pray you; if you would do me this favor, accept from me this gift, for to see your face is like seeing the face of God, and you have received me favorably. (33:10)[6]

Jacob's speaking of seeing the face of God in both of these encounters connects the two meetings in ways that I will discuss more fully in Chapter 6. The relationship between the two episodes is clear enough no matter how the respective passages are translated, although the verbal similarities between them in the original Hebrew can be made more or less obvious by the translation.

On the other hand, Jacob's thoughts on preparing his gift for Esau reveal the central importance of "seeing the face" and suggest the particular significance attached to this expression—but the prominence of this theme in Jacob's thoughts is not as evident in the translation I cited above as it is in the original Hebrew. For convenience, here is the passage once again in the JPS translation:

> For he reasoned, "If I propitiate him with presents in advance, and then face him, perhaps he will show me favor." And so the gift went on ahead, while he remained in the camp that night. (Genesis 32:21–22)

And here is the same passage in my translation with the relevant Hebrew phrases included in brackets:

> For he thought, I will appease him [AKaPRa PaNaV] with the gift that goes before me [LêPaNai] and then I will face him [lit. "see his face," PaNaV], perhaps he will favor me [YiSA PaNai]. And the gift passed before him ['aL PaNaV], and he was going to sleep in the camp that night.

The Hebrew word for "face," PaNiM, appears in the forms for "his face" and "my face" five times in this short passage. The terms "his face" and "my face" alternate with each other, underlining the idea that the face-to-face nature of the impending meeting is what looms large in Jacob's mind. Jacob's fear is thus directly addressed in the struggle with the angel—"I saw a divine being face to face and I survived"; and this struggle, in turn, prepares him for the reunion with his brother—"For to see your face is like seeing the face of God." Jacob's naming of the site of his wrestling as Peniel/Penuel, "the face of God," is thus not incidental, but reflects his relief at having prevailed in a face-to-face encounter that presages the meeting that he had been dreading.

As we will see in Chapter 6, these face-to-face meetings represent a resolution of Jacob's problematic relationship with Esau by contrasting Jacob's direct confrontation of his adversaries with his earlier underhanded tactics. Without the reader's awareness of the repeated emphasis on "the face" in the text's depiction of Jacob's thoughts, the precise nature of his fears and the corresponding laying to rest of those fears could easily be missed. Moreover, the way the text portrays these meetings, in combination with other details that I will discuss later, suggests that the narrator views Jacob's story as a morality tale involving injustice, expiation, transformation, and redress.

Aside from the use of repeated key words, the text also makes use of plays among similar-sounding words to focus the attention of the reader on important underlying issues. Word play that extends throughout a narrative serves a twofold function. On the one hand, like the use of repeated key words, the verbal markers serve as a thread that runs through the story by giving prominence to one or more central themes. In addition, however, by transforming the key words in sequential word plays, the text charts a progression in the narrative that reflects a transformation in the relationships among the protagonists.

The word plays in the story of Jacob focus on his name. At the birth of the twins Jacob and Esau, Esau emerges first and then Jacob follows with his hand grasping Esau's heel. The word for "heel" is 'eQeB, and the second son is therefore given the name Ya'aQoB, the Hebrew for Jacob, which is assumed to derive from the word for "heel." The name Jacob thus signifies someone who follows or pursues, as Jacob does in fact later pursue his elder brother in first extorting his birthright and then stealing his blessing.

When Esau discovers that Jacob has stolen his blessing he exclaims (27:36), "His name is indeed called Ya'aQoB, for he has tricked me

(VaYa'aQBeNi) now twice," playing on other meanings of the same root that have to do with trickery and crookedness.

Jacob flees his brother's wrath and stays with his uncle Laban for twenty years. After leaving Laban and preparing for his meeting with Esau, Jacob wrestles with the angel at the Jabbok crossing—YaBoQ in Hebrew. The Hebrew for "he wrestled" is VaYeABeQ. The sneaking usurper has turned into a forthright fighter.

When the struggle is over and Jacob has the angel in his power, the angel changes Jacob's name from Ya'aQoB to YiSRaEL—Israel— which is a play on a root meaning "straight"; the crooked one has become straight.

Finally, at Jacob's dreaded face-to-face encounter with his brother, Esau embraces him—VaYêḤaBQeHu, from the root ḤBQ—thus apparently resolving the conflict between the brothers once and for all. As we will see, however, Jacob's embraces always recall the wrestling that results in the eventual supremacy of a younger brother over an older brother. It is certainly not accidental that the root for embracing, ḤBQ, appears only three times in the Pentateuch, and that all three refer to Jacob's involvement in the blessing of a younger son in preference to an older son.

Lastly, we have the use of an odd word where a more appropriate alternative could have been used. When Jacob insists that Esau accept his gift, he calls the gift his "blessing" (33:11), suggesting that what he is doing is making a kind of restitution by returning to Esau the blessing that he had stolen from him.

In sum, these observations tell us something about Jacob's fears, about the evolution he undergoes in how he lays claim to a blessing, and about his insistence on compensating Esau in some way, thereby demonstrating that he realizes that justice is on Esau's side. These do not exhaust the possible conclusions that are implicit in the way Jacob's story is told; in Chapter 6, I will discuss additional facets of the story as they are suggested by the way the text tells its tale.

My point is not that the story should be read in this way or in any other way, but that evidence from the text itself suggests a particular reading. Assumptions about Jacob's righteousness or about how or why the text was originally put together should not be permitted to interfere with what the text says, and more importantly, should not distract our attention from *how* the text says what it says.

◆ ◎ ◆

Biblical commentary and scholarship comprise a vast literature. I harbor no illusions that the ideas which I propose in this book are completely novel. I have tried to acknowledge my debts to those who suggested to me one idea or another, whether in direct conversation or otherwise. To those authors, dead or living, whose conclusions I have unwittingly replicated without citing their work, I apologize. I realize that scholarly courtesy would require that I acknowledge conclusions reached by others which coincide with mine, even when my conclusions were arrived at independently. I am appending a list—by no means exhaustive—of some works in which the authors' commentaries overlap in some respect with mine, especially in my chapters on Jacob and Joseph.[7] Since I did not make use of these in my book (the bulk of which was written in the 1970s and 1980s, before most of them appeared), I do not cite them in reference to any particular point, but rather only as works that an interested reader might wish to consult, and perhaps to compare with what I have written.

Although I would be pleased to learn that there was something here that a professional scholar could find interesting, my primary goal is to introduce the general reader to a new way of reading an old and familiar book.[8]

Notes

1. James L. Kugel, *The Bible as It Was* (Cambridge, Mass.: The Belknap Press of Harvard University Press, 1997) and *How to Read the Bible: A Guide to Scripture, Then and Now* (New York: Free Press, 2007).

2. See the two books by Kugel cited above, as well as Marc Zvi Brettler, *How to Read the Jewish Bible* (New York: Oxford University Press, 2007).

3. Kugel, *How to Read the Bible*, 145.

4. For some examples of this kind of commentary see E. A. Speiser, *The Anchor Bible Genesis: A New Translation with Introduction and Commentary*

(Garden City, N.Y.: Doubleday, 1986), and Adele Berlin and Marc Zvi Brettler, eds. (Michael Fishbane, consulting ed.), *The Jewish Study Bible: Jewish Publication Society Tanakh Translation* (New York: Oxford University Press, 2004). For an example of a more strictly literary approach see Robert Alter, *The Art of Biblical Narrative* (New York: Basic Books, 1981).

5. *Tanakh—The Holy Scriptures: The New JPS Translation According to the Traditional Hebrew Text* (Philadelphia: Jewish Publication Society, 1985), 52.

6. Ibid., 52–53.

7. Besides the references cited above and in the main text, the following books contain many insightful observations: Martin Buber and Franz Rosenzweig, *Scripture and Translation*, trans. Lawrence Rosenwald with Everett Fox (Bloomington and Indianapolis: Indiana University Press, 1994); Michael Fishbane, *Text and Texture: Close Readings of Selected Biblical Texts* (New York: Schocken Books, 1979); J.P. Fokkelman, *Narrative Art in Genesis: Specimens of Stylistic and Structural Analysis* (Assen/Amsterdam, The Netherlands: Van Gorcum, 1975); Everett Fox, *The Five Books of Moses: A New Translation with Introductions, Commentary, and Notes* (New York: Schocken Books, 1995); Shmuel Klitsner, *Wrestling Jacob: Deception, Identity, and Freudian Slips in Genesis* (Jerusalem and New York: Urim Publications, 2006); Nahum M. Sarna, *The JPS Torah Commentary: Genesis* (Philadelphia, New York, and Jerusalem: Jewish Publication Society of America, 1989); Devora Steinmetz, *From Father to Son: Kinship, Conflict, and Continuity in Genesis* (Louisville, Kentucky: Westminster/John Knox Press, 1991); and for readers of Hebrew, Yehuda Kiel, *Daat Mikra: Bereshith* (Jerusalem: Mossad HaRav Kook, 1997).

8. All translations from the original Hebrew are my own, except where noted. I consulted the JPS translation when in doubt and often followed its lead, but departed from it when I thought a different rendering was preferable.

Acknowledgments

I BEGAN THIS BOOK MORE THAN THIRTY YEARS AGO, thanks in large part to what I learned about reading the Book of Genesis from David Sykes, a friend who later served as a professor of Jewish Studies for a number of years and who is now devoting his efforts to other pursuits. We first met in 1972 at Yeshivat Mir, a seminary in Jerusalem. Our earliest conversations took place at the Yeshiva and at Hebrew University when we were both young men, barely out of our teens, and were spurred by David's insights into how Genesis told its stories. Specifically, he was discovering patterns in the narratives that were reinforced by the repetition of a particular word or word root or group of numbers. This was not the first time that verbal and numerical connections had been suggested to play a role in the stories—such connections have been pointed out by many commentators, beginning with the authors of the ancient Midrashim—but his systematic approach to how these narrative tools were utilized in Genesis enabled him to point out new ways of understanding some of the texts. His work was published in his doctoral dissertation some years after our conversations took place.[1]

My first attempt at an interpretation of the Book of Genesis, dealing with the story of Jacob, was put on paper in 1977, and I continued writing sporadically for the next three decades. I benefited from David's comments on this first sketch, as well as from his reading in 1989 of a much fuller version of what would eventually become this book. Although we arrived at some similar conclusions independently, I readily acknowledge my tremendous debt to his pioneering work. I refer the interested reader to David's dissertation.

I also had the benefit of extremely helpful comments and suggestions from my late colleague James H. Schwartz and from Carla

Sulzbach. I am indebted as well to Rabbi Abraham Lieberman for his careful reading of the manuscript and for his comments and advice; to Rabbi Nathaniel Helfgot for reading portions of the manuscript and for his suggestions; to Marc Brettler for reading and commenting on the manuscript; and to my wife, Vivi, for her painstaking and meticulous copy editing.

Notes

1. David K. Sykes, *Patterns in Genesis* (Ann Arbor: University Microfilms International, 1985).

Guide to transliteration of Hebrew into
Latin characters used in this book.

The pronunciations are the closest equivalents in English.

Consonants

Translitera-tion	Hebrew Letter	Name	Pronunciation in Modern Hebrew
Uppercase Vowel	א	Alef	Can be any vowel
B	ב	Bet	B or V, depending on position
G	ג	Gimel	G as in *gold*
D	ד	Dalet	D
H	ה	He	H
V	ו	Vav	V
Z	ז	Zayin	Z
Ḥ	ח	Het	Ch as in *Bach*
T	ט	Tet	T
Y	י	Yod	Y
K	כ	Kaf	K or Ch, depending on position
L	ל	Lamed	L
M	מ	Mem	M
N	נ	Nun	N
S	ס	Samekh	S
'	ע	Ayin	Originally pharyngeal; now like Alef
P	פ	Pe	P or F, depending on position
Ṣ	צ	Tsade	Ts
Q	ק	Qof	K
R	ר	Resh	R
Š	שׁ	Shin	Sh
S	שׂ	Sin	S
T	ת	Tav	T

Vowels

A	as in *ah*
E	as in *red*
Ê	an indistinct unstressed vowel ("schwa"), like second vowel of *comet*
I	as in *deep*
O	as in *or*
U	as in *food*

The Alphabet of Creation

CHAPTER 1

Frameworks

THE FIRST THREE VERSES OF THE BOOK OF GENESIS are familiar to virtually everyone in the King James translation of 1611:

In the beginning God created the heaven and the earth. And the earth was without form, and void; and darkness was upon the face of the deep. And the Spirit of God moved upon the face of the waters. And God said, Let there be light: and there was light.

A modern translation[1] reads as follows:

When God began to create heaven and earth—the earth being unformed and void, with darkness over the surface of the deep and a wind from God sweeping over the water—God said, "Let there be light"; and there was light.

These two versions of the first lines of the story of the Creation differ in a number of ways, some merely stylistic, others matters of more substance—such as "a wind from God" that replaces "the Spirit of God"—but the two translations are clearly versions of the same original Hebrew text.

After this story of the Creation is complete, another creation story begins (2:4–7):

When the Lord God made earth and heaven—when no shrub of the field was yet on earth and no grasses of the field had yet sprouted, because the Lord God had not sent rain upon the earth and there was no man to till the soil, but a flow would well up from the ground and water the whole surface of the earth—the Lord God formed man from the dust of the earth. He blew into his nostrils the breath of life, and man became a living being.[2]

This second story is not simply another version of the first account. One of the most obvious differences between the two narratives is that the Creator is always called "God" in the first account, while He is always called "Lord God" in the second. Many other differences between these two accounts, including narrative disagreements and consistently different linguistic usages, led scholars beginning in the eighteenth century to conclude that the text as we have it is a conflation of narratives from more than one source. This "Documentary Hypothesis" was based not only on the two Creation accounts, but also on systematic differences among the various narratives in the Pentateuch which suggested that the whole of the Pentateuch is a patchwork of texts originating from a number of separate documents.

The scholarly, or archaeological, question of single or multiple sources of the text, important as it may be, is not the sort of question that I will be addressing directly. What I propose instead is to demonstrate the existence in the Book of Genesis of narrative frameworks comprising a loose architecture that cuts across the boundaries suggested by the Documentary Hypothesis. Such frameworks function as a kind of connective tissue—not only within individual stories, but also between two or more stories—and even tie together the entire book in some ways. My aim is not to argue for or against any particular view of the origins of the text, but simply to see what the book that we now have before us can tell us.

Thematic Architecture

The unifying frameworks in Genesis are of two kinds. The more conventional one, by modern standards, has to do with narrative development in the sense that later events and situations are consequences or developments or echoes of earlier ones. Thus, for example, the passive character of the second Patriarch, Isaac, has its roots in the actions and personality of his father, Abraham, the charismatic founder of a new religion. The weakness of Isaac, in turn, allows outside influences to endanger the nascent tradition of Abraham in the development of *his* sons, with significant consequences for the continued transmission of Abraham's legacy to the next generation and beyond. Accompanying the developments in the lives of the characters is a change in the nature of the relationship between God and human beings that parallels the interactions among the human protagonists.

Echoes of one account that reverberate in other accounts are created by introducing narrative patterns or paradigms with a small number of elements, and then making use in different stories of the same elements with variations on the basic paradigm. For example, the account of Adam and Eve in the Garden of Eden (Genesis 2) institutes a pattern that involves ignorance and knowledge, blindness and seeing, nakedness and clothing, and the misleading of a man by a woman who is his sexual partner. Specifically, before they eat the fruit of the Tree of Knowledge of Good and Evil, Adam and his wife are naked but are not ashamed. After the serpent persuades the woman to taste the fruit, she gives it to Adam and he eats it also. Immediately, "the eyes of both of them were opened" and they make themselves rudimentary clothing. God rebukes them for their disobedience by condemning the man to earn his living by the sweat of his brow and the woman to suffer pain in childbirth and to be subservient to the man. In later incarnations of the paradigm, besides a man being misled by a woman, it is sometimes a father who is misled by his children, or by a combination of his children and his wife.

The paradigm first set up in the story of the Garden and the Tree of Knowledge next appears in the story of the Flood in Genesis 9. After the waters of the Flood have receded, Noah plants a vineyard and gets drunk on the wine that he makes of its fruit. Unaware of what he is doing, he takes off his clothes in his tent. His youngest son, Ham, sees him, but rather than doing anything to restore his father's dignity, he simply goes out to tell his brothers what he has seen. The brothers take a garment and, walking backward so as not to see their father's nakedness, cover him. When Noah awakens from his stupor, he punishes the descendants of Ham with a curse of subservience to the descendants of his brothers.

In the story of Noah, the grapevine takes on the meaning of a Tree of Ignorance in contrast to the Tree of Knowledge. By drinking the wine that he makes of its fruit, Noah is carried back to a primeval Edenic state in which he loses his self-awareness and takes off his clothes. Noah's reclothing and Ham's curse of servile status recall the clothing of Adam and Eve after their consumption of the fruit of the Tree of Knowledge and the curses of hard labor and subservience that God imposed on the man and on the woman, respectively. There are several other places in Genesis where variations on this paradigm occur, and we will discuss them as they arise in the various narratives.

Another narrative technique highlights aspects of the protagonists' roles or the implications of their actions by periodically introducing significant objects to signal motifs that play a central role in a given story. For example, wells and altars are associated with Abraham, the first of the Patriarchs; stones play a prominent role in the story of Jacob; goats are associated with the theme of deception and betrayal that first appears in the story of Jacob and continues into the story of Joseph; clothing plays a critical role in the story of Joseph.

Verbal Structures

The second type of unifying architecture is based on verbal techniques that depend to a great extent—but not exclusively—on certain properties that are characteristic of Hebrew. Interrelations among parts of a story, sometimes demonstrating an evolution of a person or a relationship, are reinforced by the repeated invocation of terms built on a single underlying word root or by multiple word plays among similar roots. The exegetical genre of Midrash makes frequent use of similar techniques in interpreting its Scriptural sources, although not always in ways that contribute to the understanding of the plain sense of the texts. The verbal connections noted in classical Midrash tend to be local in the sense that a word or phrase in one context is cited in relation to the same word or phrase in another context, even though the relationship between the two contexts is often tenuous. By contrast, what we will do below is follow sequences of verbal markers that clarify a theme or mark a progression within a single narrative or among several narratives.

One biblical technique in particular may at first appear strange to readers of prose (but not of poetry) written in English, because it is based on the way that words are built in Semitic languages like Hebrew. In this technique, cross-links between narrative elements are constructed by using the consonantal skeletons of words in word plays, sometimes in relatively straightforward puns and sometimes by rearranging consonants to yield words interconnected by the similarity of their component sounds. How these verbal techniques work is described in the following paragraphs.

Words in Hebrew are put together by starting out with a root of (usually) three consonants and then interpolating vowels and adding prefixes and suffixes to convey different meanings derived from the root. This feature of the language is also reflected in the writing system, which is not a complete alphabet in the European sense, but a system in which the vowels are generally omitted. For example, starting with the root DBR, one of whose meanings is "to speak," interpolation of different vowels gives DaBeR, "speak" (masculine singular imperative); DiBeR, "he spoke"; DaBaR, "word," "matter," or "thing"; DiBuR, "speech"; and so on. As in other inflected languages, additional syllables are used for conjugating verbs or for forming the plural and the possessive forms of nouns, for example. Thus, DiBRa, "she spoke"; DiBaRTi, "I spoke"; TêDaBRu, "you (pl.) will speak"; DêBaRiM, "words" or "things"; DêBaReNu, "our words." The language is put together in such a way that both speakers and readers are generally much more aware of the underlying root structures of words than is the case for users of English.[3]

The Hebrew use of consonantal roots that have only three elements has two important consequences for biblical literary technique. The first is that since the number of such roots is strictly limited, there are many roots that have multiple meanings, greatly enhancing the possibilities for puns and plays on words. Thus, continuing with our example, other words built on DBR mean "to lead or to pasture" and the related "wilderness" (MiDBaR, an ownerless place of pasture), "bee" (DêBoRa), "pestilence" (DeBeR), and "sanctuary" (DêBiR). The second consequence is that other permutations of the same three consonants, or similar ones, will often also yield meaningful forms. The sensitivity of users of Hebrew to the underlying consonantal scaffolding then permits connections among such words to be perceived. Continuing further with DBR, we note that BaRaD, "hailstones"; RaBiD, "necklace"; and perhaps DaRBaN, "oxgoad," are built on roots that are permutations of DBR, and are all combinations of sounds that could be used for purposes of word play on the root for "to speak." The point is that the possibilities for word play among roots of many different meanings are numerous, and, as we will see, these possibilities are indeed often utilized.

An analogy in English to the type of word play that is used extensively in the Hebrew Bible would be the use of a series of words like "parental," "paternal," "prenatal," and even "preternatural," to link different parts of a narrative. Except in special cases, such as some of the work of James Joyce, this is a not a technique that is widely used in English prose. Because English is not built like Hebrew, attempts at the kinds of word play used in the Hebrew Bible might not work very well in English. Imagine, for example, a prose writer using a series of words like "speak," "speck," "aspic," "inspect," and so on to unify a narrative. A reader of English would, more likely than not, not notice that the writer was trying to achieve a special effect of any kind, and even if this effort were pointed out, the reader would probably be puzzled by the technique. Nonetheless, this is exactly the kind of word series that is used, and to good effect, in several of the stories in Genesis.

In the story of Joseph, for example, there appears a constellation of words built on the roots NKL ("to conspire"), MKR ("to sell"), NKR (with two meanings: "to recognize" and "to be strange or foreign"), and KMR (in a construction meaning "to pity") that runs through the narrative and charts the progression in the relationship between Joseph and his brothers. We will see in greater detail in Chapter 7 how these word plays help to tell the story of Joseph. We will point out similar examples of this kind of verbal play in other stories as they arise.

A widespread and instructive example of the power of connections forged with roots that are, or appear to be, related is the rationalization of given names in the manner of folk etymology. The first man, Adam, is so named because he comes from ADaMa, "earth." The first woman is called IŠa because she comes from IŠ, "a man." Adam later names her ḤaVa, the English Eve, because she will be the mother of all "living beings," ḤaY. ("V" [the letter *vav*] originally pronounced "W", and "Y" [the letter *yod*] substitute for each other in different constructions from the same root.) This change in name signifies her changed role. At first (2:18), she serves simply as a companion for the man ("it is not good that the man is alone, I will make him a help-mate"), so her name is understood as simply the feminine form of the word for "man." Later on (3:20), when the first humans acquire the awareness of mortality by eating the fruit of the Tree of Knowledge of Good and Evil, the man gives her a new name that reflects her role as the mother of future humanity.

The naming of the sons of Jacob in Genesis 29, 30, and 35 offers a long series of punning explanations, some of which play on more than one root in relation to a single name. For example, the birth of the sixth son of Leah is recorded in the following way (30:20): "Leah said, God has given me a good gift (ZêBaDaNi . . . ZeBeD), now my husband will dwell with me (YiZBêLeNi) for I have borne him six sons, and she called his name Zebulun (ZêBuLuN)." These namings hint in a poignant way at the unfulfilled longings of each of the sisters: Leah, the elder, hopes that the children she bears will bring her husband Jacob closer to her, while Rachel, who already has Jacob's love, longs for children of her own.

These etymologies need not be historically accurate—as if we were to maintain that the word "man" comes from the word "human," or vice versa—but bring to our attention underlying relationships and themes that are important in the narratives. Furthermore, whenever an explanation of a name is offered in the Hebrew Bible, a semantic relationship alone is not sufficient, and a phonetic relationship incorporating a similar-sounding root must be embedded in the explanation. The etymology cannot be supported by a coincidence of meanings without a coincidence of sounds as well.

There are many examples of this type of rationalization of given names. Although one must take care not to overindulge in this kind of explanation of names, there are instances where the relationship is not made explicit but can be inferred from the context. In addition, over and above the simple explanation of why a person was given a particular name, there are extended plays on the name in the account of the life story of that individual. These plays serve as a commentary on the character as a whole, often in ways that are quite complex and fraught with irony. The following examples illustrate some uses of word plays involving names.

In the stories of the second and third Patriarchs, Isaac and Jacob,

31

names serve to define the characters through the judicious use of plays on the roots underlying the names. The Hebrew for Isaac is YiṢḤaQ, from the root ṢḤQ, meaning "to laugh." The root ṢḤQ in different constructions at several points in the life story of Isaac tells us in different ways that his character lacks the *gravitas* possessed by his father, Abraham; this aspect of Isaac's character affects the transmission of the legacy of Abraham to the following generation. In addition, the same root is used to point out the inadequacy of two other potential heirs of Abraham who are passed over in favor of Isaac. We discuss Isaac at length in Chapter 5.

Jacob's Hebrew name, Ya'aQoB, is played upon more freely in the story of his life to tell us something about how his character and reputation develop in the course of his adventures. At the start, Ya'aQoB is understood to originate in the root 'QB in its meaning of "heel" and "following." As the story unfolds, another meaning of the root, "deceit" or "trickery," emerges as a result of some less-than-honest dealings on the part of Jacob. Further developments refer to similar-sounding roots with meanings of "wrestling" (ABQ) and "embracing" (ḤBQ) as Jacob prepares to face the brother whom he had earlier cheated. And there are further plays on the themes of struggle and embrace in Jacob's dealings with other members of his family. The story of Jacob is dealt with in detail in Chapter 6.

These extended verbal plays are examples of a technique of recruiting significant constellations of related or similar roots in order to reinforce some aspect of what is already implicit in the story. In some cases the constellations consist of repetitions of a single key word—not necessarily always in a single grammatical form—to drive home one salient aspect of the narrative; the story of Isaac and the account of the murder of the male children at the beginning of Exodus (see Chapter 8) are constructed with the help of this type of constellation. In other cases, plays on similar roots are used to chart the progress of the story; the stories of Jacob and Joseph contain constellations of this type (Chapters 6 and 7). The narratives in all these cases use two parallel methods to tell their tales; in addition to simply recounting the events in question, the narrative structures are mirrored in the verbal structures that carry them.

The use of consonantal patterns to construct the puns and word plays that inform the narratives bears a formal kinship with the way that the narrative paradigms which we discussed earlier are developed and played upon at a different level. In both cases we have a small number of elements that are used repeatedly in different combinations and permutations to create links among parts of a single narrative or among different narratives. The play of the paradigms can be seen as an analog, writ large, of the verbal play.

Other ways in which the force of the narrative is buttressed by its verbal structure are illustrated in the Creation accounts, as I will show in the next chapter. We will see there that attention must be paid to the precise forms of the words used as well as to the structure of individual sentences. In addition, the manner of linking sentences into units, by formulaic repetitions or other devices, is an instrument for charting one or another type of narrative progression.

We have now been exposed to a portion of the literary armamentarium of the Book of Genesis. I will have occasion to point out examples of the use of some of these same techniques in later books of the Pentateuch as well. And further, we will also see how the authors of later books—I will use examples from the Books of Joshua and Ruth—picked up some of the same paradigms and used them for their own ends, indicating that these later authors were familiar with the techniques used in the earlier books.

Having said this much about some of the formal and structural aspects of the Book of Genesis, the time has come to wrap up this abstract discussion and to begin to read the book itself.

Notes

1. *Tanakh—The Holy Scriptures: The New JPS Translation According to the Traditional Hebrew Text* (Philadelphia: Jewish Publication Society, 1985), 3.

2. Ibid., 4–5.

3. For those who are familiar with Hebrew, I should point out that in order to highlight the consonantal root, I will generally transcribe Hebrew words with the consonants in capitals and the vowels in lower case. I will follow this procedure even in cases where the orthographic convention includes a written indication of the vowels; thus, I write "she spoke" as DiBRa and not DiBRA or DiBRaH, despite the presence of a final "H" in Hebrew to specify

the vowel. Conversely, I will capitalize vowels when they follow *alef* in order to show that the *alef*, which is not indicated in an obvious way in the English transliteration, is an element of the root. I will not distinguish the geminated form of a consonant (doubling of the consonant, indicated by the *dageš ḥazaq*) from the simple form, nor the stopped form (indicated by the *dageš qal*) from the fricative (or spirant) form of the same phoneme. That is, the stops B, K, P, and T will not be distinguished from their respective fricative forms V, KH, F, and TH, since the distinction between the stopped and fricative forms is a later development. In any case, neither gemination nor spirantization is reflected in the orthography.

See the table on page 21 for a summary of the transliteration used in the book and a guide to the approximate pronunciation of the transliterated Hebrew.

PART ONE

Creation and Knowledge

CHAPTER 2

The Creation of God and the Creation of Man

W E BEGAN CHAPTER 1 BY NOTING THAT THERE ARE two accounts of the Creation at the beginning of the Book of Genesis, and that these accounts differ so significantly that scholars concluded that they must have come from two different sources. No matter how one accounts for the presence of the two stories, the specific ways in which they differ all converge to indicate that these accounts present the world from two different perspectives. These two perspectives continue to be represented throughout Genesis, and the interplay between them is one of its underlying concerns. In this chapter, I will discuss the two Creation stories and show how their respective views of the Creation are implied in their accounts of how the world originated.

The Two Views of the Creation

The two perspectives—at once opposed and complementary—that inform the two Creation stories are, on the one hand, that of an omniscient God and, on the other, that of a human whose perception is limited by space and time. We will see this opposition maintained throughout in our close reading of the texts. The problems of whether and how the protagonists of the later stories of the Patriarchs become aware of God's role in the events taking place around them occupy a central place in the book. Human awareness of God's participation in the affairs of mortals evolves as the narratives unfold, while the nature of communication between God and humans evolves in a parallel manner. These interactions between the perspectives of God and of human beings constitute a major theme of the Book of Genesis.

As we read the two Creation stories carefully, we will see in detail how the two perspectives are presented. We begin with the first of the two stories.

The first account of the Creation starts out with the following familiar description of the world on the first day:

> At the beginning of God's creation of the sky and the land, the land was unformed and void and there was darkness over the depths, and God's wind [or "breath" or "spirit"] was hovering over the waters. God said, Let there be light; and there was light. God saw that the light was good, and God separated between the light and the darkness. God called the light Day and the darkness He called Night; and it was evening and it was morning, one day. (1:1–5)[1]

These lines set the initial conditions, the setting in which God begins to act. In this account, there is at first formlessness and darkness, wind and water. What is lacking is form and structure. Fittingly, therefore, God begins to order the world—at first visually—by creating light and separating it from darkness. This is the first of a series of creations and separations that result ultimately in the physical world as we know it. Order is also introduced in a more subtle way, by means of God's structuring activity expressed in a highly structured narrative. I will have more to say about the verbal structures later on.

In the second account, a structured world is presupposed at the very start:

> No shrub of the field was yet on the land and no grass of the field had yet grown, for the Lord God had not caused it to rain on the land and there was no man to work the earth. (2:5)

This account anticipates itself in projecting forward to a state of affairs that exists now but did not yet exist then. It describes the initial scene by telling us about the shrubs and grasses that had not yet sprouted, the rain that had not yet fallen, and the not-yet-created man who was not yet working the land. The frame of reference is the world as we now perceive it (emphasized by "yet" in the text), whereas the first account began with a state of affairs that can only be imagined, a state of undifferentiated formlessness and void. Furthermore, the frame of reference of the second account, in contrast to the first, is explicitly anthropocentric. What is missing is vegetation, because there had been no action on the part of God to enable it to grow, and there was no man to work the land. Man is absent, both as an efficient cause (there was no vegetation because there was no man to make it grow) and also as an end, or final cause (there was no vegetation because there was as yet no man for whom it would be of use). Man is a central determinant in the second account as he was not in the first.

The fundamental difference in frame of reference between the two stories is expressed also in the different orders of creation. In the first version, the man is created on the sixth and last day of the Creation, only after everything else has been completed (1:27). Thus, he could not, even in principle, have been a witness to the Creation. Not so in the second, where the man is the very first thing whose creation is told:

> A mist rose from the land and watered all the surface of the earth. The Lord God formed the man of dust from the earth, and He blew the breath of life into his nostrils, and the man became a living soul. The Lord God planted a garden in Eden, in the east, and He placed there the man that He had formed. (2:6–8)

The man was present at the subsequent creation of all the other living creatures. In the first account of the Creation, there were no eyewitnesses outside of God Himself, and the story is therefore prehistory in the strictest sense of the word. In the second Creation narrative, the man is at least a potential eyewitness to the events related—a fact that renders these events a part of history proper.

There is thus a fundamental difference in the way the man became aware of the two Creations. He could understand the first in a limited sense by inference and extrapolation from the completed world into which he was born. In the second Creation story, by contrast, he was already present when God planted the trees in the garden and when the other living creatures were made. The first process of creation was known only by God; the second could be known by the man as well. This dichotomy lies behind many of the other differences between the two accounts that will become clear as we continue.

The first Creation is seen with the eye of God; the second with the eye of man.

Divine Structure and Human Understanding

Let us now look at the first account in more detail:

At the beginning of God's creation of the sky and the land, the land was unformed and void and there was darkness over the depths, and God's wind was hovering over the waters. God said, Let there be light; and there was light. God saw that the light was good, and God separated between the light and the darkness. God called the light Day and the darkness He called Night; and it was evening and it was morning, one day.

God said, Let there be an expanse in the midst of the water and let it separate between water and water. God made the expanse, and it separated between the water that was above the expanse and the water that was below the expanse, and it was so. God called the expanse Sky, and it was evening and it was morning, a second day.

God said, Let the waters below the sky gather into one place and let the dry land appear, and it was so. God called the dry land Land and the gathering of waters He called Seas, and God saw that it was good.

God said, Let the land bring forth plant-life . . . and it was so . . . and God saw that it was good. And it was evening and it was morning, a third day.

God said, Let there be lights in the expanse of the sky to separate between the day and the night . . . and it was so . . . God made the two great lights . . . and God saw that it was good. And it was evening and it was morning, a fourth day.

God said, Let the waters teem forth swarms of living creatures, and let birds fly in the land over the face of the expanse of the sky. God created . . . and God saw that it was good . . . And it was evening and it was morning, a fifth day.

God said, Let the land bring forth living creatures each according to its kind . . . and it was so. God made . . . and God saw that it was good. God said, Let us make mankind in our image and likeness, and they will rule over the fish of the sea and the birds of the sky and the animals and over all the land and over all the creeping things that creep on the land. God created the man in His image, in the image of God He created him, male and female He created them . . . and it was so. God saw all that He had made and it was very good, and it was evening and it was morning, the sixth day.

The sky and the land and all their hosts were completed. On the seventh day God completed all the work that He had done, and on the seventh day He ceased from all the work that He had done. And God blessed the seventh day and made it holy, for on it He ceased from all the work of creation that God had done. This is the story of the sky and the land when they were created. (1:1–2:4)

The structure of the narrative is very obvious. The work is divided among six days, each of which is marked by the beginning formula "God said, Let such and such happen . . ." and, with some variations, continues with "God made (or created) . . . , and it was so . . . , and God saw that it was good," and closes with "And it was evening and it was morning, an nth day."

There is an additional structuring of the work of the first six days into two parts, each comprising a unit of three days. In the first unit God sets up the various realms, or spaces, that make up the universe; in the second, He populates each realm with its proper inhabitants.[2] The creation of light and its separation from darkness on the first day is completed by the creation on the fourth day of the two heavenly lights that separate light from darkness, and of the stars; the separation of the two waters by the sky on the second day is completed by the bringing forth of the water-creatures and the birds on the fifth day; and the appearance of land and vegetation on the third day is completed by the bringing forth of the land-creatures on the sixth. The man, last to be created on the sixth day, is told to rule the living creatures—"the fish of the sea, the birds of the sky, and all the living things that creep on the land."

Curiously, however, the structural unity of the narrative is the only kind of unity that it possesses. There are no explicit links between one segment of God's activity and the next. We are given no clue, for example, why, after separating light from darkness, God went on to separate the two waters. Nor, for that matter, are we told what motivated God to do any of the things He did in the first place. And, in fact, what at first appears to be a reason, or perhaps a justification, for God's actions—the formulaic "And God saw that it was good" that punctuates the story—serves to isolate the sections of the narrative from one another by implying a self-sufficiency of each part of the Creation without reference to any of the other parts.

The same phrase—"And God saw that it was good"—also lends a celestial loftiness to the account that is reinforced in other ways. In what sense was the result of God's particular activity good? Good for what? The use of "good" in this way seems to carry connotations that are more esthetic than anything else—it is a goodness that is not linked to a function or to any other practical or moral standard of value. "Good" means "good in the eyes of God."

Loftiness is further evoked in the abstractness of God's actions during those six days. The verbs used to denote those acts are not descriptive of a clearly defined manner of acting; they are not concrete. In this account, God "creates," "makes," "says," "sees," "separates." In Hebrew, as in English, none of these verbs has any intrinsic relationship to its object. Thus, the verbs "create" or "make" or "separate" can be followed by arbitrary objects. The verbs are general, and thus serve to keep their subjects remote from their objects. The differences between these verbs and those that describe God's actions in the second Creation story will make this idea clearer.

God's actions as they are named in the second account, by contrast, are specific and concrete. He rains, models from the earth, blows breath into man's nostrils, plants a garden, causes trees to grow, puts the man to sleep, and takes one of his ribs, from which He fashions a woman—after first making certain to close up the place on the man's body from which He took the rib (Genesis 2). The words that describe these actions are explicit with respect to how exactly they were performed and specific with regard to their objects. For example, what translates into English as "caused it to rain" is a single word in Hebrew, derived from the root meaning "rain," so that one could translate the phrase in verse 5 as "because the Lord God had not yet rained upon the earth." The other verbs are similarly evocative of exactly what it was that God did in any particular instance.

A similar point can be made with respect to the products of God's activities. The products of God's creativity in the first chapter of Genesis are not the objects of everyday concern that are subject to coming into being and passing away, but are rather those components of the perceptible world that are either permanent or self-perpetuating. In the second account, the objects are not the cosmic entities of the first Creation, but are local and specific in their relation to daily human concerns. Let us quote here a bit more of the second account in order to make the contrast more apparent:

> The Lord God caused to grow from the earth every tree that is pleasant to look at and good for eating, and the Tree of Life was in the middle of the garden, and the Tree of the Knowledge of Good and Evil. A river came out of Eden to water the garden, and from there it separated into four branches. The name of the first is Pishon, and it encircles all the land of Havila, where the gold is. The gold of that land is precious [lit. "good"], bdellium and onyx stone are there. The name of the second river is Gihon, and it encircles all the land of Kush. The name of the third river is Hidekel [Tigris], and it goes to the east of Ashur; and the fourth river is the Prat [Euphrates]. (2:9–14)

In the first account God created "the land," not a garden set in a particular location in Eden, in the east, as described in the second; "the seas," rather than the four explicitly named rivers that flow in specific countries; "trees and grasses" generically, rather than the Tree of Life situated in the midst of the garden, and the Tree of Knowledge of Good and Evil. The words used to name God differ in an analogous way in the two stories. In the first, He is simply "God" (ELoHiM), a word signifying power or dominion that is used of other powers as well, both mortal and immortal; in the second, the proper name of the God of Israel, translated as "the Lord," is used.

The words that describe God's actions in the second account are not only concrete, but are in addition the same terms that are used to describe human work. Thus, the actions convey the tactile sense of manual work that is lacking in the first version, and also serve to define in yet another way the perspective of the second account—the perspective of a human observer for whom the meaning of the Creation lies in its explicit relatedness to human concerns.

God's actions in the first story, like the structure of the story itself, are characterized by their formality. He makes binary separations, defining the limits of light and darkness, heaven and earth, sea and land. And He gives names to the newly delimited entities: Day and Night, Sky, Land and Seas.

Plants and animals are defined as to species, each reproducing according to its kind; the lights in the sky separate day from night and light from darkness, and serve as signs for the temporal divisions, days and years; each of the three realms of heaven, earth, and sea has its own denizens; and man, created male and female, in God's image, is set as ruler over them all.

A further indication of the focus of the first account is revealed when we take even a cursory look at its syntax. Most of the sentences and clauses are of the form "And God did such and such," repeated formulaically again and again. First of all, the repeated use of this structure adds to the formal character of the whole that we have already noted. Secondly, this syntactic arrangement suggests that just as God is the grammatical subject of the sentences, so might we consider the subject of the narrative to be, in a sense, God Himself rather than the Creation. The Creation, with its binary divisions and progressive demarcations of realm from realm, is thus no more than an expression of God as a creator—in this case, God as the architect of a system with a particular kind of logical structure. Definition, in both the literal sense of marking limits and in the extended sense of verbal definition—or naming—is what this Creation is all about.

That this creation process is primarily a discursive process of categorization and definition is demonstrated by the fact that it proceeds by means of speech alone. God says "Let there be light," or "Let there be a separation," rather than actually fashioning or modeling whatever He wishes to create. When the text writes that "God made" or "God created" in any specific instance—with one exception—the phrase is always preceded by "God said, Let such-and-such occur"; God makes and creates simply by saying. What is created in this way is a rational universe, a world that can be defined by language and thereby becomes an object of knowledge. The characteristic activity of God in this text is definition, and from the activity we infer the nature of the actor.

The one exception to the principle of creation through speech is the creation of the man. Here God begins by speaking, as in the other acts of creation, but rather than saying "Let there be a man" or "Let the earth bring forth a man," He says "Let us make a man in our image and likeness," and then proceeds to the actual creation of the man. Nevertheless, the creation of the man is still not like the concrete and craftsmanlike makings of the second Creation account. And it is also important to note that, unlike the other living beings, the man is not said to be made from the earth or the water. These differences between the creation of the man and that of the rest of the universe imply that he is different from the rest of the Creation in that he is not simply another component of an orderly universe, but a being who has a special place in it and who has dominion over the earth and its creatures. God personally makes the man, unlike the other creatures, who are brought forth from the earth or the water. But in spite of his special status, the man remains a part of the divinely ordered hierarchy.

The God in whose image the man is created, according to this reading of the first Creation account, is the God who ordains the structuring of an orderly universe on rational principles. The man is a creature for whom the world can be an object of understanding, just as the Creation is—in the sense we suggested above—the playing out of a logical process by God. This is not to say that the man's only role is as a being who can know the world, and through it, God, but since in the first account of the Creation the world is described in its aspect of a knowable order—as the product of a logical structuring process—it is the man's relation to this kind of world, and to the kind of God who brought it into being, that is revealed.

Cosmogony and History—Division and Integration

After telling the story of the six Creation days, the first account continues to the seventh day, when God has completed His work of creation. The emphasis placed on the fact that God completed and "ceased from all the work that He had done" implies an absolute separation between the preceding story and all that follows. The work of the Creation is finished now and, after the separation of the six Creation days of divine history from all later events by the seventh day, human history begins in the second Creation narrative. It is at this juncture that the name of the divinity changes. Whereas before He had been called generically "God," He is now called "Lord God," a term that includes the proper name of the God of Israel by which He introduces Himself to Moses in the Book of Exodus. The first God is the God of Creation; the second, although also a God of Creation, is principally the God of human history as well, and more specifically, the God of Jewish history. Thus, the second account of the Creation is the real beginning of history as we know and participate in it.

Let us quote here the continuation of the second account:

> The Lord God took the man and placed him in the Garden of Eden to work it and to guard it. And the Lord God commanded the man and said, You may eat of all the trees of the garden. But from the Tree of the Knowledge of Good and Evil do not eat, for on the day that you eat of it you will die.
>
> The Lord God said, It is not good that the man is alone; I will make him a fitting helpmate. The Lord God fashioned from the earth all the beasts of the field and all the birds of the sky and He brought them to the man to see what he would call them; and whatever the man called each living thing, that is its name. The man gave names to all the cattle, the birds of the sky, and all the beasts of the field, but for the man no fitting helpmate was found.
>
> The Lord God cast a deep sleep on the man and he slept, and He took one of his ribs and closed up the flesh underneath it. The Lord God built the rib that He had taken from the man into a woman, and He brought her to the man. The man said, This one now is bone of my bone and flesh of my flesh, this one will be called Woman [Iša], for she was taken from a man [Iš]. This is why a man leaves his father and his mother and cleaves to his wife, and they become one flesh. (2:15–24)

The second account, in contrast to the first, is an integrating narrative in the sense that there are explicit interrelations among the components of the world. The structure of the second account is thus not formal, but intentional (in the sense of "meaning-endowing"). Directly following the statement about the absence of vegetation, for example, are the reasons for this absence: God had not caused it to rain, and there was no man to work the land. On this background we read the first statement of God's activity: "The Lord God fashioned the man of dust from the earth."

There are two points to notice here. First, the creation of the man is a response to the state of affairs that existed earlier—there was no vegetation because there was no man; therefore a man was made. The man's creation is motivated by the world in the sense that we could understand his creation as being necessary for the growth of the plants. The second point is an extension of the first one to a more concrete level: The man is not said to be created in the image of God, as in the first account, but is molded by God from the dust of the earth. The man is thus *of* the world in a physical sense. And there may even be a suggestion that the man is made of all parts of the world—the dust of the earth, watered by the mist, inspired with the breath of life (2:6–7)—evoking the tri-partite nature of the world as earth, water, and air or sky.

The narrative continues with God planting a garden and placing the man in it. The implied motivation again points back to man. God creates the garden for the man. We know that it is for the man because of what follows: "The Lord God caused to grow from the earth every tree that is pleasant to look at and good for eating, and the Tree of Life was in the middle of the garden, and the Tree of the Knowledge of Good and Evil" (2:9).

All of the things created in the second account are explicitly related to man, whereas in the first account none of the products of Creation until the very end of the story had any explicitly stated connection with humanity. When God completed the Creation in the first account, He gave the plants to man for food; but man is not distinguished from the other animals in this—the plants serve as food for all the animals. In a sense, therefore, even this action to supply a human need is simply one more aspect of the order that God brought out of the primal formlessness.

There are other contrasts to the first Creation account in the story of the planting of the garden. In Genesis 1, the plants were described with respect to their differentiation into species and their capacity for propagation—"And the land brought forth vegetation, all kinds of grasses that bear seeds and all kinds of trees that bear fruit with its seed in it" (1:12); here, in the second account, they are defined in terms of their human importance ("pleasant to look at and good for eating"). In the first account, the adjective "good" in "And God saw that it was good" separated the different parts of the Creation from one other by implying the self-sufficiency of each of the portions of Creation; here, when the text tells of trees that are "good for eating," the word functions in exactly the opposite way, now linking the trees to man by noting their usefulness to him. Thus, the word "good" in the first account is abstract—even enigmatic—while in the present account it has explicit reference to human needs.

God then places the man in the garden, to work it and to tend it. We see here once more the reciprocity that holds between the man and the garden. The garden has a function with respect to the man, but the man also has a function with respect to the garden. God then permits the man to eat the fruit of the trees of the garden, with the significant exception of the Tree of the Knowledge of Good and Evil.

But, the narrative continues, the man was alone—he needed a helpmate. Here is a second instance of the use of the word "good" in relation to a human need: "It is not good that the man is alone." God brings the animals to the man to see whether any of them can serve as a helpmate for him, but none is found suitable. Consequently, out of the man's own flesh, God makes a woman to serve as his helpmate. The recounting of the Creation here has an internal coherence that is entirely lacking in the first version.

The anthropocentricity of the second account is evident, as we noted earlier, in that the verbs used are those that describe human activities—modeling, planting, building. Similarly, the rivers and lands in 2:10–14 have the names of specific geographical and political entities, and the products—gold, bdellium, onyx—of those lands have meaning only in terms of human standards of economic and esthetic value.

A most telling contrast appears in what may be a deliberate reference to the first account in the second. Great weight is given to God's speech in the first account, where the Creation is actually carried out by means of God's utterances. Further, God reserved for Himself the naming of the eternal components of the universe—Day and Night, Sky, Land and Seas—in the first three days of Creation. But when it came to naming the living creatures in the second Creation account, He deferred to the man. Definition here belongs to the man, not to God. And in fact, the man's role extended further than mere naming, since it was ultimately to him that God left the choice of an appropriate companion. The joint role of the man with God is adumbrated in the second sentence of this account as well, for the reasons that are given for the absence of plant life are twofold, and are given equal weight—God had not yet caused rain, but, in addition, there was no man to work the land. Man in the second story is a creator too, both by his naming and by his assigning of significance to the things and events of the world.

To summarize: Where the first account is formal and abstract, the second is informal and concrete; where the structure of the first is determined by the logic of definition and differentiation, the second is informed by a logic of intention and integration; where the first has as its focus a God who creates a universe ordered according to a principle of discursive reason, the second describes a world in which man is both an integral component and a prime determinant. Thus, while the first account concerns a knowable or inferable world, the second tells of a world defined by man's perceptions, needs, and desires. In the most general terms, the first account has as its reigning idea that of separation and distance, while the second is ruled by integration and connection. The universe of Genesis 1 is presented from the perspective of God and is characterized by a particular kind of structure; the world of the second account, by contrast, is seen with the eyes of man and is therefore characterized by its interconnected meanings.

A Human Perspective of God

A difficulty that we must meet in this interpretation of the two Creation accounts concerns the perspective of God. What does it mean to look at something through God's eyes? How can we know God's perspective? The "point of view of God" can only be the perspective of God as imagined from the perspective of man. The first Creation account is therefore characterized by its parsimoniousness, in the sense that nothing is postulated beyond what is in principle immediately accessible. Thus, there are neither motives given, nor explanations offered, for the largely undescribed activities of God during the first seven days. It is an account that is phenomenological and behavioristic; we see only results, without really knowing how they were achieved. The results of God's activities imply a certain orderliness in Creation, but they do not justify this order.

This parsimoniousness can be understood in two different ways. A more conservative understanding of the text's failure to attribute motives to God could follow from the recognition that whatever God's motives are, man may not be privy to them and should therefore not presume to burden God with the products of his own imagination. This understanding can be thought of as a kind of humility in the face of a greater design: Who are we to say why God acts in any particular way?

But a more radical understanding of the parsimoniousness of description of God's actions is possible, and this understanding involves the recognition that to speak of God as having motives at all can be no more than a metaphor, like, at a different level, "the hand of God" or "the face of God." This recognition follows from the realization that meanings as we understand them are human productions, just as perceptions are human productions. The point is that God is radically, fundamentally, different from mortals, and although we can perhaps say something about Him by extrapolating from the results of His activity that are available to us, what we can say is not really very much. The only attribute that the first Creation account chooses to impute to God, by implication, is a kind of logic that is related to the formal aspects of thought and language. To impute motives to God would overstep the limits of what we actually perceive.

The second Creation account has many links among its different parts, all of them tending to embed man inextricably in the world. In the second account, it is the man who names the animals, and it is his needs and perceptions that color the description of the created world, including the description of the creator's actions. The reciprocity that holds at the level of man's physical interactions with the world is mirrored in an implied reciprocity at the level of man's knowledge of the world—in particular with regard to meaning. The world is still a given in the sense that it is God who actually does the work of creation, but it is now man's needs and his naming that define the world. And this definition by man extends even to God Himself, in that God's activities are presented as cosmic versions of the activities of human craftsmen, with discernible motivations underlying them. In the first account there is no such reciprocity between God and His Creation—the world is an emanation of God—while in the second account the comprehensible nature of God is a reflection of man's concerns.

The second Creation story is the beginning of history. We may infer, therefore, that the view of God and history implied in this story applies equally to all of the history that follows. The aspect of the story that is most important for all later events is the understanding of human history in terms of God's involvement in it. That God intervenes in human affairs is amply documented in the rest of the Book of Genesis, as well as in the rest of the Hebrew Bible, but perhaps the perception that meaning is a human creation should also be applied to the recounting of later history. Thus, perhaps everything that is asserted about God and His actions should be understood purely as human interpretation, rather than as a body of absolute statements about God. Indeed, our understanding of the first Creation account implies that absolute statements about God cannot be made.

The two complementary accounts of the origins of the world serve as an introduction to what follows. On the one hand, man should be aware that he cannot impute meaning to God absolutely; nevertheless, the interaction of God with the human world is given meaning by man. And this meaning is given, not as the result of any choice on man's part, but simply as a consequence of his nature—for, just as it is the nature of the human eye to see, so it is the nature of the human mind to perceive meaning. And, further, just as the character of what is seen is determined by the eye, so the character of meaning is determined by the mind.

Reading and Creation

There are other implications of the two Creation accounts, implications that concern the reading of the text. On our understanding of the Creation accounts, we are presented with two perceptions of the world: the Creation as an emanation of the character of God and, alternatively, as a world informed by human meanings. The first world is one of which we can stand in awe, and in which we can participate insofar as we share God's nature. But the second world—the world of desire and need, of work and pain—is the world we *live* in. The presentation of these accounts side by side tells us that the two worlds are one. The rest of the Book of Genesis is an elaboration of the theme of human awareness—or ignorance—of God's role in the human world.

The two ways of seeing the world of Creation apply also to reading the text of the Creation—or any other text, for that matter. There are many ways in which one can participate, or choose not to participate, in a text. The way of the second Creation account is the one we have been pursuing until now; it is the determination of the text through meanings imparted by the reader. In reading, we create the text, albeit not *ex nihilo*—our meanings are not simply arbitrary impositions on the text. This way of reading is the reciprocal involvement of a reader and a text that concerns him in the same way that the man in the second Creation account watered and tended the garden that nourished him.

The second Creation account is the real beginning of human history, and the rest of the Hebrew Bible is a continuation of this account, a history seen through human eyes, where meanings—even the meanings of God's actions—are nonetheless human meanings. If we pursue the analogy between understanding the world and reading the text, we can now say that the rest of the book should also be read in a participatory manner. We should allow ourselves to enter the text as we recognize that we are not merely readers, but also contributors to the meaning of the narratives.

With this in mind, I invite the reader to enter the Garden.

Notes

1. I will not justify my choice among the different possible translations for any given word or phrase unless some critical point hangs on the choice. Nonetheless, I will try to be consistent in rendering occurrences of a given Hebrew word by a single English equivalent. Thus, EReṢ will be "land," ADaMa "earth," and so on.

2. See U. Cassuto, *A Commentary on the Book of Genesis (Part I): From Adam to Noah*, trans. Israel Abrahams (Jerusalem: Magnes Press, 1961), 17, 42.

CHAPTER 3

Knowledge Unacknowledged: The Tree and the Serpent

THE STORY OF ADAM, EVE, AND THE SERPENT, THE Tree of Knowledge of Good and Evil and the Tree of Life, is certainly one of the best known—if least understood—stories in the Bible. Various doctrines about original sin, the fall of man, the perniciousness of sex in general, and of woman in particular, have all been derived from this tale. What these and practically all other interpretations have in common is the view that this is a story about sin and punishment. I believe that this emphasis is mistaken. I think that the story means to present us with a definition of what we are, rather than focusing on what we did to deserve to be that way. The Creation stories tell us about essential aspects of the world and our understanding of it by describing how the world and its creatures originated. In the same way, the story of the Garden of Eden defines what it means to be a human being—as opposed to God, on the one hand, and to the beasts of the field, on the other—through a tale of origins.

Knowledge and Life, Death and Birth

Among the trees that God planted in the Garden of Eden were the Tree of Life and the Tree of Knowledge of Good and Evil. Two questions that come to mind on reading the story of Adam and his wife in the Garden are, first, what exactly is the knowledge of good and evil that eating of the Tree of Knowledge imparted? And second, what, if any, is the connection between the two magical trees? Broader questions are: What is the story doing in this place in Genesis, and does it

53

have any relation to the rest of the book? I will offer some suggestions in the way of answering the first two questions before going on to address the place of the story in the context of the whole book.

The story of the Tree of Knowledge has commonly been taken to have a sexual significance, as referring to a loss of innocence of sexual matters. Although this may be obvious, it is enlightening to see how a careful reading of the whole of the second Creation account shows precisely how the text presents the unfolding of sexual knowledge. At the same time, however, sexual knowledge is only one of the many interrelated themes of the story.

As we saw in our preceding chapter, a comparison of the two Creation accounts is the best way to discern the critical aspects of each of them. When we make such a comparison, we see that the second account differs from the first in the complete absence of any reference to reproduction or sexuality. In the first account, we read about seed-bearing plants that propagate according to species, about the blessing to "be fruitful and multiply" (applied both to animals and to humans), and about the creation of two genders. All of these are missing from the second account. The creation of the man and of the woman in the first account reads as follows:

> God created the man in His image, in the image of God He created him, male and female He created them. God blessed them and said to them, Be fruitful and multiply and fill the land and conquer it . . . . (1:27–28)

In the second account, the man is created alone:

> The Lord God said, It is not good that the man is alone; I will make him a fitting helpmate. The Lord God fashioned from the earth all the beasts of the field and all the birds of the sky and He brought them to the man to see what he would call them; and whatever the man called each living thing, that is its name. The man gave names to all the cattle, the birds of the sky, and all the beasts of the field, but for the man no fitting helpmate was found. (2:18–20)

The animals are not created in pairs as sexual partners, as in the first account, but are brought individually to the man to be his companions, with no mention of the partner that the man would need in order to reproduce. When, finally, the woman is created from the man's rib, there is still no intimation of sexuality, or of procreation:

> The Lord God cast a deep sleep on the man and he slept, and He took one
> of his ribs and closed up the flesh underneath it. The Lord God built the
> rib that He had taken from the man into a woman, and He brought her to
> the man. The man said, This one now is bone of my bone and flesh of my
> flesh, this one will be called Woman [IŠa], for she was taken from a man
> [IŠ]. This is why a man leaves his father and his mother and cleaves to his
> wife, and they become one flesh. (2:21–24)

The man names her IŠa—Woman—because of her creation from
IŠ, a man, exactly as the man was called ADaM because he was created from ADaMa, the earth. And to emphasize the absence of sexuality from this Creation, while at the same time anticipating what will
follow, Genesis 2 concludes, "The two of them were naked, the man
and his wife, but they were not ashamed" (2:25).

This last sentence suggests what might be the true significance of
the absence of references to sexuality in the account up to this point.
It is not that there is no sexuality, but rather that it lies outside, or
beneath, the awareness of the man and the woman. They are naked,
but they are blind to their own nakedness.

The story of the serpent and the eating of the fruit of the Tree of
Knowledge of Good and Evil follows. The human pair then discover
that they are naked; ashamed, they make themselves rudimentary
clothing. God rebukes them:

> To the woman He said, I will make the suffering of your conception great;
> in pain will you bear children, and your desire will be to your husband,
> and he will rule over you. To the man He said, Because you obeyed your
> wife and ate of the tree which I told you not to eat of, may the earth be
> accursed on your account; with suffering will you eat of it all the days of
> your life. It will grow thorns and thistles for you, and you will eat the grass
> of the field. By the sweat of your brow will you eat bread until you return
> to the earth, for from it were you taken, for dust are you and to dust will
> you return. (3:16–19)

For the first time now the human couple hears of two related phenomena, childbirth and agriculture—the seed of man (ADaM) and of
the earth (ADaMa). But the relation between the man and the earth
is even closer. Not only is the man told that he will be forced to wrest
his sustenance from the earth, but he is also told that he himself—like
the grass of the field—comes from the earth and, even more momen-

tously, will in the end return to it. Just at this point—just as he learns of both birth and death—the man sees his wife with new eyes and gives her a new name: "The man gave his wife the name Eve (ḤaVa), for she was the mother of all living beings (ḤaY)." ("V," originally pronounced with the sound of "W," commonly interchanges with "Y" in many words.) So, just as the role of giver of names has passed from God to man, so too the role of creator is now shared with humans.

The end result of eating of the Tree of Knowledge of Good and Evil is awareness of birth and death, and recognition of the role of the woman as mother rather than simply as companion. Awareness of death leads to the discovery of life, and thus to the desire for life. The focus consequently shifts to the Tree of Life, necessitating the expulsion from the Garden:

> The Lord God said, Now the man has become like one of us to know good and evil, and now he is liable to reach out and take also from the Tree of Life, and eat, and live forever. And the Lord God sent him out of the Garden of Eden to work the earth from which he had been taken. (3:22–23)

The choice of words is precise—the man is sent to work the earth "from which he had been taken," echoing the last words of the curse, ". . . until you return to the earth, for from it were you taken . . . ." It is only now, after the man has named his wife ḤaVa—the mother of all living beings (ḤaY)—that God fears that the man will eat of the Tree of Life (HaḤaYiM) and live (VaḤaY) forever. Now that humans have become aware of their own power in creating new life, they must understand that this power remains limited, and that, although the humans can approach God in their knowledge of good and evil, they cannot contend with Him in the temporal domain. Despite the fact that Eve is now the mother of all living beings, the life that she can bestow and the life that God retains in His realm of the Tree of Life remain forever separate; this separation is assured by the return of the man to the earth from which he was taken.

The next practical consequence of eating the fruit of the Tree of Knowledge is given in the first verse of Genesis 4: "The man knew Eve his wife, and she conceived and bore Cain . . . ." This verse is a condensation of what had been determined in the Garden of Eden. We can translate the verse more literally, paying attention to the implied relationships among the earth, the man and the woman, life and creation: "The man (he of the earth, ADaM) knew Eve (the life-giver, ḤaVa), his wife (she of the man, IŠa), and she conceived and bore Cain (the created one, QaYiN)." The special use of the verb "to know" in its sexual sense is introduced here with reference to the Tree of Knowledge; the text deliberately names the man's wife in order to juxtapose knowledge and life, in reference to the two trees; and she conceives and bears a son, as God had ordained for her in the Garden after the couple ate of the Tree of Knowledge. Remarkably, when Eve gives birth to her first son, she calls him Cain—QaYiN—because "I have created (QaNiTi) a man with God," a statement that hints at Eve's secret thought that her achievement is commensurate with God's. This child of hubris becomes the first destroyer of a man, the murderer of his brother Abel. Eve, although truly a life-giver, cannot contend with the one who controls the Tree of Life. When her son Seth, the replacement for the dead Abel, is born, Eve is more circumspect in her naming (4:25): "She called him Seth (ŠeT), for God has given me (ŠaT) other seed in place of Abel, for Cain had killed him."

Good and Evil, Desire and Fear

The context in which the Tree of Knowledge appears includes many matters of major importance. In God's response to the eating of the fruit we hear about birth, pain, corporeality, death, toil, agriculture, the psychology of the sexual relationship; that is, about virtually all the important issues of human existence. Sexuality is only one facet of the greater story.

There is a common aspect to all of the phenomena revealed to the humans after they eat the fruit of the Tree that explains why this knowledge is called the knowledge of good and evil, and that also explains some of the singular aspects of this knowledge. The knowledge of good and evil acquired by eating the fruit is the awakening of a new awareness of the two forces that govern human life, the forces of attraction and repulsion that make life possible and define it—good and evil are the objects, respectively, of desire and fear.

Desire has two faces: One is hunger, the driving force for individual survival, and the other is sexual desire, the force that ensures survival of the species. These desires are innate and instinctual. But desire is not the only force that fosters survival; fear of injury and death is the other. This fear, too, is innate and instinctual. Common to all of these instincts—implicit in their being instincts—is that they are blind: They are not propelled by any conscious awareness of their consequences. Hunger and sexual desire are not predicated on the consciousness of their ends. We do not eat because we know that we will die if we do not eat; similarly, sexual desire does not arise from the wish to reproduce. These desires are ignorant of their ends. In the same way, fear of death is not a fear that is aware of its true object. We do not need to think of death in order to be paralyzed with fear as we peer over the edge of a precipice.

A related dichotomy inheres in the distinction between eating the fruit of a tree and sowing seeds in the ground. We stretch out our hand and take a fruit to satisfy our hunger now; by contrast, we plant crops not because we are hungry, but because we know that if we do not sow now we will starve later. As long as they were in the Garden, the man and the woman ate the fruit of the trees; after they were driven out, they were nourished by what they sowed.

The knowledge that came with eating the fruit of the Tree of Knowledge of Good and Evil is the knowledge of the consequences, or the ends, or the aims, of these blind instincts. At some point in the evolution of human consciousness we, as a species, came to understand that our bodies are made of the same dust as the earth and every other body, that reproduction follows upon sexual intercourse, that each of us will eventually die—just as each of us learns these truths at some time in our individual development.

These are curious truths, in a number of ways. First of all, none of us witnesses our own birth or our own death. As a corollary, at the deepest levels of our awareness we cannot really believe in our own non-existence, just as we are not really aware of ourselves as assemblages of meat and bone, or atoms and molecules. What is more, the ideas that our flesh is not very different from the flesh of the cattle which we eat, and that we will someday die, are repugnant to us. We actively do not wish to know these facts—we cover this knowledge from ourselves.

All of these facets of our self-awareness are things that we know and do not know, at one and the same time. This paradoxical awareness arises from our confrontation with an order of reality that is non-human, a reality that encompasses both what we share with other instinct-driven beings and what we share with beings that have no life at all. We are not equipped to assimilate a reality that is non-human, but this is what we try to do when we step outside of our instincts and grasp their real meanings. As a result, our attempt is not completely successful—we can think the consequences of our instincts, but it is only our instincts themselves that we can feel. Our understanding of where our desires and fears tend does not actually do much in the way of moderating them—the instincts remain instincts, no matter how we may rationalize them. However, it is our understanding that leads us to attempt to channel these instincts and fears in various ways. The totality of these attempts, beginning with clothing, is what we call civilization. Our attachment of purpose to the blind forces that drive us is the foundation of what we call morality—one of the meanings of the biblical Good and Evil—because it is only when we are able to step outside of our instincts that we can attain the self-awareness that is necessary for any morality.

This understanding is expressed in the equation of "Good and Evil" with "Life and Death," since life and death are what lie behind desire and fear once we properly comprehend these innate drives. In understanding the purposes of our instincts we become like God—we transcend ourselves in being able to see ourselves from the outside, from above. We become knowers of life and death, and no longer merely beings that live and die. But, at the same time, this knowledge also diminishes us when we realize that we are not essentially different from the dust that we come from. Here we run up against the same problem that we encountered in the two Creation stories—there are two orders of reality that course side by side, a non-human reality within which we are blind and have no understanding, and a human reality which we create out of the non-human by giving it meaning and purpose. But our creation of this reality is flawed, because we know that we are the ones who create it, and that the gap between it and the non-human remains in truth unbridgeable.

Knowledge of All Things—Even Death

It is possible to understand the events in the Garden in another way, closely related to the first, but with more of an emphasis on the knowledge of mortality in particular. This second approach also leads to different ways of understanding the knowledge of good and evil. Let us look more closely at the story now:

> The two of them were naked, the man and his wife, but they were not ashamed.
> The serpent was the most cunning of all the beasts of the field that the Lord God had made. He said to the woman, So, God has said that you should not eat of any of the trees of the Garden, has He? The woman said to the serpent, We may eat of the trees of the Garden. But of the tree that is in the middle of the Garden God has said, Do not eat of it and do not touch it lest you die. The serpent said to the woman, You will not die; for God knows that on the day that you eat of it your eyes will be opened and you will be like God, knowers of good and evil.
> The woman saw that the tree was good for eating, and that it was a delight to the eyes, and that the tree was desirable for making one wise [meaning uncertain], so she took of its fruit and ate, and she gave to her husband with her also, and he ate. The eyes of the two of them were opened, and they knew that they were naked, so they sewed fig leaves and made themselves loincloths. (2:25–3:7)

Then God enters the picture:

> They heard the sound of the Lord God walking in the Garden in the day-time breeze, and the man and his wife hid themselves from the Lord God among the trees of the Garden.
> The Lord God called to the man and said to him, Where are you? He said, I heard Your sound in the garden and I was afraid because I am naked, and I hid. He said, Who told you that you are naked? Did you eat of the tree from which I had forbidden you to eat? The man said, The woman that You placed with me, she gave me of the tree, and I ate. The Lord God said to the woman, What is this that you have done? The woman said, The serpent enticed me, and I ate.
> The Lord God said to the serpent, Because you have done this, may you be accursed above all the cattle and all the beasts of the field; you will walk on your belly and you will eat dust all the days of your life. I will set hatred between you and the woman and between your seed and her seed; he will strike your head and you will strike his heel. (3:8–15)

Then, after God's rebuke to the man and to the woman that we quoted earlier:

> The Lord God made tunics of skin for the man and his wife, and He dressed them. (3:21)

God's message to the man ends with "For dust are you and to dust will you return" (3:19). This is an astounding piece of information. More than the fact of being a body and being subject to death, it is the *knowledge* of these facts that is so momentous. Gaining an awareness of mortality is in an important sense the loss of immortality: ". . . except for man, all creatures are immortal, for they are ignorant of death."[1] The fact of mortality permeates our lives only because of our knowledge of it; it is only when we attain the awareness of death that death becomes our master. This is the meaning of God's warning to the man that on the day that he eats of the Tree of Knowledge he will surely die. This is why the question in the Garden is not simply of death itself, but rather of the knowledge of death. This is why it is the tree of this knowledge that stands in opposition to the Tree of Life— the Tree of Knowledge is really the Tree of Death. When the man and the woman are afterward barred from being able to eat of the Tree of Life, this is no more than the other side of acquiring the knowledge of death—by knowing that we are mortal we lose immortality.

Immediately after this revelation to the man, he renames his wife— from Woman she becomes Eve, the "mother of all life." The woman, who is the bringer of the knowledge of death, is also the bringer of life. Or perhaps the opposite is more accurate: By showing the man that life has a beginning, the woman teaches the man that life is not limitless—that just as life has a beginning, so it can also have an end. Before Eve appears, the man has no intimation of either birth or death; birth and death only become real when there are others whose experience we can observe. The role of sexuality is transformed as a result of the knowledge of death, since it now is recognized to be the only way of circumventing mortality. Thus, at the same time that death is acknowledged, the means for defeating it are also recognized—for just as life has an end, so it can also have a beginning. Sexuality is thus recognized both as an expression of corporeality and as a transcending of corporeality.

The special nature of this knowledge of the limits of life is conveyed through the role of the serpent and the motifs of nakedness and covering. The figure of the serpent in its symbolic richness incorporates a number of the central themes of the story of the Garden. First of all, the serpent is lethal. And so, the serpent in the Garden fulfills his role as a bringer of death. The serpent is also a common sexual symbol. There is a particular context for all of the appearances of the serpent in the narratives of the Pentateuch. In the story of the Garden, the serpent appears in connection with trees, the Tree of Knowledge of Good and Evil and the Tree of Life. He returns in Exodus, in the magical transformation of the staff of Moses—the staff on which Moses leans for support—into a writhing snake, and then back into a staff (Exodus 4). And in Numbers 21, when God visits a plague of venomous serpents on the grumbling Children of Israel, Moses sets up a brass serpent on a pole to save the people. The deadly serpent is always associated with a life-sustaining tree or staff. The association of the serpent and the staff may have a sexual significance as a metaphor for male sexual potency. In all the instances of the appearance of serpents, a tree, or staff, or pole, is ancillary to life or support, while the corresponding serpent symbolizes death and destruction. The fact that the symbols appear in pairs, corresponding to life and death, supports the idea that the focus of the story of the transgression in the Garden—expressed partly in imagery that is sexual—is primarily on matters of life and death. The transformation of the staff into the serpent and back again is the shift between sexual potency and its opposite; it is also the corresponding shift from life to death, and—characteristic of the serpent, as we will see in a moment—from death back to life.

The deadly serpent carries an additional association, with deceit or guile, ideas that are related to hiding and covering. He bites in the heel, from behind, unseen. This is part of God's curse on the serpent—men will strike the serpent's head, while he will strike men in the heel. Likewise in the foretelling of the future of Jacob's son Dan, the Patriarch says: "Dan will be a serpent on the road, a viper on the path, who bites the heels of the horse, and his rider falls backward" (Genesis 49:17).

The guile of the serpent in his seduction of the woman in the Garden is related to knowledge in a further sense, in that he is able to deceive her by means of knowledge that he has and that she lacks: "The serpent was more cunning than all the beasts of the field." The Hebrew word that is translated as "cunning" in the last sentence is 'aRuM. The immediately preceding verse in the narrative tells us that the man and his wife were naked, but felt no shame; the word that means "naked" is 'aRuMiM, the plural form of 'aRuM. The juxtaposition of the guile of the serpent with the innocence of the humans is ironically underscored by this word play, as if to say that the humans were so naive that they could not distinguish one kind of 'aRuM from the other.

But the description of the serpent as 'aRuM, meaning both "cunning" and "naked," is an allusion to another characteristic of the serpent that carries powerful symbolic significance and that relates to another theme of the story—the serpent's ability to renew his youth by periodically shedding his old skin. This is the transformation from death back to life that was suggested by the staff/serpent duality mentioned earlier. The serpent shows himself in yet another way to be a master of death, for in addition to being able to deal it out to others, he can to all appearances stop his own progressive descent into death by shedding his old skin and repeatedly returning to a youthful nakedness. 'ARuM in its meaning of "naked" recalls 'oR, the word for "skin." The serpent discards his old skin and emerges naked, to start life over. Covering is thus associated with the decay that portends death, while nakedness signifies renewal and youth. It is this perpetual youth that is lost to the man and the woman after they eat the fruit of the tree.

The significance that was attached to the molting of the serpent in the ancient Near East is attested in the Babylonian epic of Gilgamesh. The hero of the epic goes to seek the secret of immortality from Utnapishtim, the man whom the gods have made immortal. Before Gilgamesh leaves the abode of Utnapishtim, the immortal discloses to him the place where a plant that can restore youth is to be found:

> Gilgamesh, I shall reveal a secret thing, it is a mystery of the gods that I am telling you. There is a plant that grows under the water, it has a prickle like a thorn, like a rose; it will wound your hands, but if you succeed in taking it, then your hands will hold that which restores his lost youth to a man.

63

Gilgamesh finds the plant, but then loses it before he can make use of it:

> Gilgamesh saw a well of cool water and he went down and bathed; but deep in the pool there was lying a serpent, and the serpent sensed the sweetness of the flower. It rose out of the water and snatched it away, and immediately it sloughed its skin and returned to the well. Then Gilgamesh sat down and wept, the tears ran down his face.[2]

The serpent combines attributes of death and eternal youth, of sexuality and the circumventing of death by procreation, and he is insidious—he creeps up when man is unaware, like death itself. But the insidiousness of the serpent is more than the insidiousness of death, for there is nothing that is more insidious than the knowledge of death.

Our awareness of mortality arises at some time in our childhood or early youth. But, as we saw earlier, our awareness of our own mortality only rarely takes root in our consciousness; even though we are nominally cognizant of the inevitability of our own eventual death, we never really believe it. We are, in this sense, as ignorant of mortality as were Adam and Eve in the Garden. The fact that the man and the woman cover themselves suggests their concealing of this knowledge from themselves, as we all continually do. We know that we are mere dust—muscle, fat, and bone—and we know that we will die, but we push this knowledge from ourselves, we do not wish to know it. God's making for the man and woman garments of skin ('oR, a play on 'aRuM) is a favor He bestows on them in the guise of an imperfect return to their earlier state of innocent nakedness. They are, indeed, covered, but their covering is only of skin, and as such is a kind of secondary nakedness. They thus become ignorant once again—as before, they no longer see their nakedness—but their acquired ignorance is ambiguous in a way that their original ignorance was not. Whereas before they had not been ashamed because the sense of shame was alien to them, their lack of shame now is contingent on their being covered—on their forgetting.

The Tree of Knowledge of Good and Evil is thus connected with the unique recognition that we have of our being subject to death.

We may still ask, however: If this knowledge is knowledge of bodily decay and death, why is it called the Knowledge of Good and Evil?

There are several possible answers to this question. The first and probably the simplest is, as I suggested earlier, that "Good and Evil" means "Life and Death." The knowledge that then sets men apart from the beasts is the grasp of the facts of death and life. This is our ability to see the limits of life even as we are immersed in a life that feels to us limitless.

The phrase "Good and Evil" can be understood in two other senses on the basis of its appearances elsewhere in the Hebrew Bible, and can be understood to be related to death in two correspondingly different ways. The first sense is simply "everything" or "anything" or "all manner of things"; this knowledge, then, has a cognitive connotation. In this case, the correct formulation, rather than "Good and Evil," would be "good and evil," or "good and ill." When the servant of Abraham comes to find a wife for his master's son in the land of Haran, the girl's brother and father tell him: "This matter is from the Lord, we can say neither ill nor good to you" (24:50), meaning that nothing they can say will affect the outcome of his quest, since it has been ordained by God.

If the phrase in the name of the Tree in the Garden is taken with this meaning, then we must understand this general knowledge as resulting in the recognition of mortality. What is at issue then is the growth of the knowledge of the man and the woman into realms that had earlier been inaccessible to them. In this sense, then, the phrase carries the implication that the price of a sophisticated consciousness—a knowledge of all things—is that it extends even to the awareness of death, with all its consequences. Thus, the knowledge of the world that is characteristic of divine beings ("you will be like God") reaches even to the limitations of the human knowers themselves. This knowledge, by expanding the world of humanity, causes humanity itself to contract in its own eyes.

The second sense of the phrase "Good and Evil" is the more conventional one that relates to questions of moral judgments of right and wrong. How is this kind of knowledge related to the knowledge of death? I would venture that our moral sense is predicated in a profound way on our awareness of our mortality, for it is our mortality that makes for the irrevocable character of the consequences of our actions. Ethical judgments would have little meaning for immortal beings, since the significance of any action, considered from the perspective of infinite time, would be infinitely diluted. In the first way of understanding the knowledge of good and evil, knowledge of mortality is the unavoidable price that must be paid for an expanded awareness; in this second way, an expanded awareness—a moral awareness—is a consequence of the knowledge of mortality.

Woman and Life

No matter how we understand the knowledge that came with eating the fruit, there is a common underlying meaning. The knowledge that the man attained through the woman is knowledge of himself. And the later expression of knowledge as carnal should be taken very literally, for by "knowing" the woman—who is literally his flesh—the man comes to know his own flesh. He can recognize what he is only when he sees himself as another creature, from the outside.

The interaction between the man and the woman in the Garden serves as a model for the other relationships between men and women in Genesis. The woman is created to be "a fitting helpmate" for the man (2:18). The Hebrew is 'eZeR KêNeGDo, which translates literally as "a helper opposite him" or "a helper against him." In truth, this phrase expresses exactly the role of many of the women in Genesis, who help their men—or at least set them straight—in spite of themselves. In these relationships the women and the men are at cross-purposes as a result of differing perceptions and desires, and the role of the women is to force an unwelcome reality on the reluctant men. The women are characteristically the initiators of the action, the men are usually unaware of how they are being influenced, and covering and uncovering with clothing are important. The final, and perhaps the most significant, element in the paradigm is the unswerving dedication of the women to the purpose of bearing and preserving their children in the face of the indifference or the opposition of the men. We will see in a later chapter that this last role is carried over into the Book of Exodus as well.[3]

66

The first story of an interaction between men and women after the expulsion from the Garden is the incestuous coupling between Lot and his daughters following the destruction of their home, the city of Sodom. For now it will suffice to summarize the events briefly: Lot's daughters believe that no men were spared in the devastation of the cities of the plain, and that they will then never be able to bear children. Therefore, in order to ensure the survival of the human race, they ply their father with wine and take advantage of his intoxication to seduce him (19:30–38). We will return to this story in a later chapter.

The next instance is the exchange between Abraham and Sarah in Genesis 21. Sarah, because of her childlessness, has given her maidservant Hagar to Abraham in a quest for at least vicarious motherhood. Hagar then gives birth to Ishmael. When Sarah subsequently has her own son, Isaac, however, she perceives Ishmael as a threat:

> She said to Abraham, Drive out this maidservant and her son, for the son of this maidservant will not inherit together with my son, with Isaac. This displeased Abraham greatly on account of his son. God said to Abraham, Do not be displeased concerning the boy and your maidservant; whatever Sarah tells you, listen to her, for in Isaac will your seed be acknowledged. (21:10–12)

After the story of Abraham, we have an account of Rebecca's manipulation of her husband Isaac and son Jacob, where the discord—recalling that between Abraham and Sarah—is a result of the fact that Isaac favors his older son, Esau, while Rebecca favors the younger Jacob. When Rebecca hears of her blind husband's intention to bless Esau, she has Jacob cover his smooth skin with goatskins to simulate the hairiness of Esau and has him put on Esau's clothing in order to trick Isaac into bestowing the blessing on Jacob instead (Genesis 27). Jacob himself had earlier extorted Esau's birthright from him by taking advantage of his elder brother when he was in a weakened state (Genesis 25).

Rebecca plays the role of the first woman in relation to both Isaac and Jacob: Not only does she instigate the deception of the passive Isaac, but she does this by covering her son Jacob—both in skins and in clothing—in order to obtain for him something that was not intended for him, like the knowledge of good and evil in the Garden. The end result, as in the Garden, is Jacob's flight from his home and, as we will see later, his acquiring of his wives and children.

The continuation of the story demonstrates how Jacob is forced to learn that birthrights and blessings can neither be bought nor stolen. Jacob flees to his uncle Laban to escape the wrath of Esau. There, he falls in love with the younger of Laban's two daughters, Rachel, and agrees to work for Laban for a period of seven years in exchange for Rachel's hand. When the seven years are up, Laban surreptitiously substitutes his older daughter, Leah, for Rachel in the dark of night after the wedding feast:

> And in the morning, behold, it was Leah! He said to Laban, What is this that you have done to me? It was for Rachel that I worked with you, and why have you deceived me? And Laban said, It is not done so in our place, to give [or "to put"] the younger before the elder. (29:25–26)

The women—Laban's daughters—are instrumental in teaching Jacob the lesson that the younger is not so easily put before the elder, that his stealing the blessing of his older brother by attempting to change places with him is not so easily pardoned.

In a later episode (Genesis 38), Judah, one of the sons of Jacob, prevents his widowed daughter-in-law, Tamar, from marrying his last surviving son. As a childless widow, she is prohibited from marrying anyone else as long as her dead husband has a living brother who can marry her. Judah has thus made it impossible for Tamar to bear a child. Tamar takes off her widow's garb, covers herself with a veil, and sets out to deceive Judah into thinking that she is a harlot so that he will lie with her. She succeeds in her plan, and becomes pregnant by Judah. When Judah learns that Tamar is pregnant, he orders that she be taken out and killed. Tamar, however, presents Judah with the evidence that the man responsible for her pregnancy is in fact Judah himself. He acknowledges the justice of her case, confessing that the responsibility for what she had done lies with him for not giving her in marriage to his son—humiliating as it is for him to be thus publicly exposed. We will discuss this story more extensively later.

Finally, we have the celebrated story in Genesis 39 of the young

Joseph and the lustful wife of his Egyptian master Potiphar. The Egyptian lets Joseph run his household, and thus effectively takes a holiday from his duties. Potiphar's wife, also abandoned to Joseph, tries to seduce the boy. When Joseph refuses to lie with her, she snatches his garment from him and displays it to her husband as evidence that Joseph tried to seduce her. She uses Joseph's garment to deceive her husband and to protect herself, demonstrating to him what happens when a man renounces his responsibilities and leaves them in the hands of someone else. At the same time, the stripping of a garment from Joseph (not the first time that this has happened to him) is a further step in his education in humility and in the precariousness of human fortunes—that is, in self-knowledge. Interestingly, this is the only case where the woman's desire is purely sexual and not a means of bringing about birth—but this is also the only instance in which the woman is responsible for removing a garment and uncovering the man, rather than using a garment to cover what needs to be hidden. Reference to birth in the Garden of Eden story comes only after clothing has been introduced; perhaps Potiphar's wife is guilty of attempting to return to a time before the knowledge of good and evil has been acquired, like her ancestor Ham the son of Noah (whom we will discuss in Chapter 4). In any case, we will also deal with this episode more fully in a later chapter.

Each of these instances of conflicts between men and women has a place within the development of the narrative of which it forms a part. Nonetheless, the general paradigm of these interactions was first set forth in the story of the Garden of Eden when the woman offered the man the fruit of the Tree of Knowledge of Good and Evil. The recognitions that are forced on the men by the women are echoes of the recognition of death—and birth—that was precipitated by the woman in the Garden.

The second Creation story posits a connection between death and the relationship between man and woman. Both death and marriage are re-unions—returns to an earlier, undifferentiated state. In the case of death, the reunion is of man with the earth: ". . . until your return to the earth, for from it were you taken, for dust are you and to dust will you return" (3:19). In the case of man and woman, the union of the two is a re-joining as well:

> The man said, This one now is bone of my bone and flesh of my flesh; she will be called Woman [IŠa], because she was taken from a man [IŠ]. This is why a man leaves his father and his mother and cleaves to his wife, and they become one flesh. (2:23–24)

The etymological explanations that are given for the naming of the man and the woman are parallel. IŠa, the woman, comes from IŠ, "man," just as ADaM, "man," came from ADaMa, "earth." Since Creation was accomplished by acts of separation, the two ways that a man relinquishes his separateness—in union with a woman and in death—must be through reunifications of what had originally been one, and only later divided.

Becoming Human

The very beginning of Genesis defined, in a general way, the distinction between the perspective of God and that of human beings. The following story of the Garden pursues the delineation of the essential features of what it is to be human. The characteristic that defines human beings is their recognition of the limits that circumscribe life, the understanding of the meaning of birth and mortality. This awareness bestows a unique significance on all man's actions and is the root of the recognition of good and evil. The knowledge that was acquired in the Garden is not shared with the animals; it is this knowledge that makes man uniquely mortal among all the beasts of the field. But at the same time that this awareness makes man alone mortal among all the animals, his grasp of the boundaries of life and death and of the distinction between good and evil also makes him like the God who built a universe by creating boundaries and distinctions in the primordial chaos.

Notes

1. J. L. Borges, *Labyrinths: Selected Stories and Other Writings*, ed. D. A. Yates and J. E. Irby (New York: New Directions Books, 1964), 114.

2. N. K. Sandars, *The Epic of Gilgamesh* (London: Penguin Books, 1960), 113–14.

3. The emphasis on the role of the women as bearers and protectors of their offspring was pointed out to me by David Sykes.

CHAPTER 4

Erasing the World:
The Flood of Noah

THE BEGINNING OF GENESIS DESCRIBED THE CRE-
ation of the world by separations—of light from darkness,
land from water, heaven from earth, man from the earth, and
woman from man. Finally, the man and the woman were removed
from the garden that God had planted for them and that held within
it the Tree of Life, to which there would be no returning. Boundaries
were set that were intended to be eternal, never to be transgressed.

What follows, however, is the erasing of those boundaries, first
by men and then by God Himself. The story of Noah tells how the
Creation was put into peril by the breaching of those boundaries, and
how they were reinstated in a newly constituted world, reconciled to
imperfection.

The Undoing of Creation

Genesis 4 and 5 present two lines of descent from Adam and Eve.
The first is the line of Cain, murderer of his brother, while the second is the line of Seth, the son who replaces the dead Abel. The first
line is presented as a summary succession following the account of
the murder of Abel: "Irad was born to Enoch, Irad begot Mehuyael,
Mehuyael begot Methushael, and Methushael begot Lemech" (4:18).
There follows a short account of the life and deeds of Lemech and the
attribution of the origin of various arts and occupations to his sons.

The line of descent of Seth, largely parallel in its names to the line
of Cain, is dealt with in a more formal and repetitive manner and at
greater length. The short biographies follow a formula:

Adam lived one hundred and thirty years and he begot [a son] in his form and image and called him Seth. The days of Adam after he begot Seth were eight hundred years and he begot sons and daughters. All the days of Adam that he lived were nine hundred and thirty years, and he died.

Seth lived one hundred and five years and he begot Enosh. Seth lived eight hundred and seven years after he begot Enosh and he begot sons and daughters. All the days of Seth were nine hundred and twelve years, and he died.

Enosh lived ninety years and he begot Kenan. Enosh lived eight hundred and fifteen years after he begot Kenan and he begot sons and daughters. All the days of Enosh were nine hundred and five years, and he died.

Kenan lived . . . and he died.

Mahalalel lived . . . and he died.

Jared lived . . . and he died. (5:3–20)

This listing is reminiscent of the first Creation account in its formulaic character. The first break in the string of short life-stories occurs with Enoch, the seventh in line from Adam, of whom it is said:

Enoch lived sixty-five years and he begot Methuselah. Enoch walked with God for three hundred years after he begot Methuselah, and he begot sons and daughters. All the days of Enoch were three hundred and sixty-five years. Enoch walked with God and was not, for God had taken him. (5:21–24)

Enoch is the only one of all the descendants of Adam whom death does not take.

The formula resumes with Enoch's son Methuselah and, with the insertion of a short notice, continues with the grandson of Enoch, another Lemech, who begets Noah:

Lemech lived one hundred and eighty-two years and he begot a son. He called him Noah [NoaḤ in Hebrew] to say, This one will comfort us [YěNaḤaMeNu] from our works and from the toil of our hands from the earth which the Lord has cursed. Lemech lived five hundred and ninety-five years after he begot Noah, and he begot sons and daughters. All the days of Lemech were seven hundred and seventy-seven years, and he died. (5:28–31)

Noah, like Enoch, is one who walked with God, alone in his wicked generation: "These are the descendants of Noah, Noah was a righteous man, perfect in his generations; Noah walked with God" (6:9).

In the preceding verse—"But Noah found favor (ḤeN) in the eyes of the Lord"—the word for "favor" is simply the inversion of the same two letters as Noah in Hebrew; the Hebrew form of Enoch (ḤaNoK) is also a play on the same root. Noah, like Enoch before him, escapes the common fate of the rest of humankind; Noah escapes the Flood, as Enoch escaped death itself.

The key to the story of Noah and the Flood is hinted at in plays on word roots related in their sound to NḤ. Hence the rationalization of the name Noah in verse 29 of Genesis 5: "This one will comfort us (YêNaḤaMeNu) from our works (MiMa'aSeNu) and from the toil (Me'iṢBoN) of our hands from the earth which the Lord has cursed." This is a reference to the cursing of the earth which followed Adam's and Eve's eating the fruit of the Tree of Knowledge of Good and Evil in Genesis 3: ". . . may the earth be accursed on your account; with suffering ('iṢaBoN) will you eat of it all the days of your life."

The naming of Noah is linked, both verbally and conceptually, to the future destruction of the human race. The passage telling of God's decision to destroy the world by a flood is striking in its parallelism to the naming of Noah:

> The Lord regretted [VaYiNaḤeM] that He had made ['aSa] man on the land and He was saddened [VaYiT'aṢeB] in His heart. And the Lord said, I will wipe [EMḤe] man that I have created off the face of the earth, from man to beast to creeping thing to bird of the sky, for I regret [NiḤaMTi] that I made them ['aSiTiM]. But Noah [NoaḤ] found favor [ḤeN] in the eyes of the Lord. (6:6–8)

The beginning of this passage includes the same three verbs that figure in the naming of Noah: NḤM, which has senses relating to both solace and regret; 'SH, "to make" or "to do"; and 'ṢB, "sadness," or "toil," or "suffering." The appearance of Noah is an assurance that the destruction will not be total. At the same time, the plays on Noah's name are all on roots that signify reversal or undoing. Thus, God regrets (NḤM) that He made the world and decides to eradicate it (MḤH), while Noah himself appears in order to mitigate the destruction; solace (another sense of the root NḤM) mitigates sorrow.

There are additional plays on words with the same and similar root letters in the story of the Flood as well. The destruction is repeatedly referred to as "wiping out" or "eradication" (from the root MḤH), the ark rests (VaTaNaḤ) on the mountains of Ararat as the water recedes (8:4), and the dove finds nowhere to rest (MaNoaḤ) on the first occasion that Noah sends it out to see whether dry land has yet appeared (8:9). At the very end of the Flood narrative, Noah offers a sacrifice to God—"The Lord smelled the sweet savor (NiḤoaḤ) and the Lord said to Himself, I will not again curse the earth on account of man . . . ." (8:21). The final reversal, God's relenting and affirmation that He will never again undo the Creation, is presented in the context of a sweet savor that is reminiscent of the name of Noah. This last in the series of plays on Noah's name represents God's forgiveness and the reconciliation that is effected between God and His Creation. We will see later how the two other series of word plays that run through the narratives of Jacob and of Joseph similarly end with a term that signifies forgiveness and reconciliation.

The theme of reversal is central to the story of Noah. The destruction of the world is carefully portrayed in a manner that makes it abundantly clear that it is a reversal of the Creation. The reason for this destruction is also given in terms of the reversal of the character of the world from God's original vision of it. In the account of the Creation we saw the phrase "And God saw that it was good" repeated again and again. The final summation of the Creation is: "And God saw all that He had made and it was very good" (1:31). In the second Creation story, God's planting of the Tree of Knowledge of Good and Evil is recounted, as well as man's eating of the forbidden fruit. This is the first appearance of the word "evil."

When, earlier, God had noted that the man was lacking a partner, He said "It is not good that the man is alone" (2:18). The world is good, or at the worst, there might be something that is not good—that is, not perfect—about it, which God immediately rectifies. The Tree of Knowledge introduces the possibility of the perception of Good and Evil.

When we arrive at the introduction to the Flood narrative we read:

And the Lord saw that the evil of the man in the land was great, and that all the imaginings of the thoughts of his heart were only evil all the day. And the Lord regretted that He had made the man . . . . (6:5–6)

75

What had started out as only good had progressed to the possibility of evil, and then, finally, to "only evil": "God saw that the land was corrupted (NiŠHaTa), for every creature had corrupted (HiŠHiT) its way on the land" (6:12). The world that God had envisioned has been corrupted. It is at this point that God decides to destroy the world. He tells Noah in the next verse that He will destroy all the living creatures—using the same root that means both to corrupt and to destroy, ŠHT. God's reversal of the Creation follows upon the reversal of the character of the Creation by the creatures themselves.

The devastation wrought by the Flood is an undoing of the Creation. Just as the waters above and the waters below had been separated in the Creation, they are now reunited:

> In the six hundredth year of the life of Noah, in the second month, on the seventeenth day of the month, on this day did all the springs of the great deep [TêHoM, cf. 1:2] split open and the gates of the heaven opened up. (7:11)

The dry land disappears, and all the land-creatures die. The world has once more become a watery void; the only break in the bleakness is the tiny ark floating on the surface of the waters—the window through which a new Creation will issue.

The next reversal is the reversal of the devastation of the Flood, a reprise of the original Creation that had been wiped out. It begins with God's remembering:

> God remembered Noah and all the animals and all the cattle that were with him in the ark, and God caused a wind to pass over the land, and the waters subsided. The springs of the deep [TêHoM] and the gates of the heavens were stopped up, and the rain was held back from the sky. The waters ebbed from the land gradually, and the waters were diminished at the end of one hundred and fifty days. The ark came to rest in the seventh month, on the seventeenth day of the month, on the mountains of Ararat. (8:1–4)

The wind passing over the water is like the wind that hovered over the water before the first Creation—"A wind from God hovered over the waters" (1:2)—and the deep (TêHoM) of the first beginning is stopped up once more at the beginning of this second Creation.

The ark comes to rest in the seventh month, perhaps recalling God's resting on the seventh day (although God's action is expressed not as resting but as "cessation," the root of which gives the word "Sabbath"). The mountains appear, Noah sends out the raven and the dove to test the habitability of the earth, and, finally, the earth dries completely. Note that in the Creation account also the first to appear were the water creatures and the birds who fly in the heavens, and only on the following day did the land creatures come onto the scene (1:20–22).

God instructs Noah to leave the ark and to take with him his family and all the animals that he had with him in the ark in order that they may once more populate the earth:

> Leave the ark, you and your wife and your sons and your sons' wives with you. Take out with you all the living things that are with you of all flesh of birds and cattle and of all the creeping things that creep upon the land and let them teem in the land and let them be fruitful and multiply on the land. (8:16–17)

This passage recalls the appearance of the living creatures on the fifth and sixth Creation days, when the creatures were generated from the water and from the earth (1:20–25).

Noah then prepares a sacrifice to the Lord, and the Lord, on perceiving the sweet savor, vows never again to destroy the world:

> The Lord smelled the sweet savor and the Lord said to Himself, I will not again curse the earth on account of man, for the imaginings of the heart of man are evil from his youth, and never again will I smite all the living things as I did. All the rest of the days of the earth will sowing and harvest, and cold and heat, and summer and winter, and day and night not cease. (8:21–22)

This is a reaffirmation by God of the orderly working of the world, a reinstitution of the order of the days and the seasons originally promulgated in the Creation. A significant difference between this summary statement and the one at the end of the Creation—"God saw all that He had made, and it was very good"—is that now a place for evil in the world is explicitly recognized and accepted.

Finally, to dispel any doubt we might still have that the account of Noah's rescue is intended to be a second Creation, we have God's blessings to Noah and his family:

> God blessed Noah and his sons and said to them, Be fruitful and multiply and fill the land. And the awe and fear of you will be on all the living things of the land and on all the birds of the sky, of all that the earth causes to creep forth and of all the fish of the sea, all are given to you. Every creeping thing that lives is yours to eat, as the green grasses have I given you all. (9:1–3)

This blessing and what follows it echo God's words to the man and woman at the time of the original Creation, with some important changes concerning what may be eaten:

> God blessed them, and God said to them, Be fruitful and multiply and fill the land and conquer it; and rule over the fish of the sea and the birds of the sky and all the living things that creep on the land. And God said to them, I have given you all the grasses that bear seeds that are on the face of all the land, and all the trees that have fruit that bear seeds, they are for you to eat, and for all the living things of the land and for all the birds of the sky and for all that creeps on the land that has life, all the green grasses are to eat; and it was so. (1:28–30)

The next few verses in the Noah story contain prohibitions concerning the eating of the blood of the animals (perhaps a reference to the Tree of Life—"for the blood is the soul," Deuteronomy 12:23) and the shedding of human blood (possibly an allusion to the murder of Abel by Cain [9:5–6]—"from his brother-man will I require a reckoning for man's life . . . for in the image of God did He make man.") And finally, once more, "And you be fruitful and multiply, teem in the land and multiply in it" (9:7).

After the blessings and exhortations to Noah, God makes a covenant with the inhabitants of the earth in the form of a rainbow stretching from heaven to earth, promising that He will never again bring a flood to destroy all life on earth (9:8–17). This episode resembles the account of God's completion of His labors at the end of the sixth Creation day in that both passages serve to separate in an absolute manner what came before from what follows. The seventh day marks the end of God's creation of the world, while the rainbow marks the end of God's destruction of the world. Neither of these up-heavals will ever be repeated.

Noah's Garden of Eden

A further development in the story of Noah of the theme of reversal of the original Creation is suggested in the following passage:

> The sons of Noah who came out of the ark were Shem, Ham, and Japheth, and Ham is the father of Canaan. These three were the sons of Noah and from them did all the land diverge. Noah began to be a tiller of the earth and planted a vineyard. He drank of the wine and became drunk, and uncovered himself in his tent. Ham, the father of Canaan, saw the naked-ness of his father and told his two brothers outside. Shem and Japheth took a garment and put it on both of their shoulders and walked backward and covered the nakedness of their father; they faced backward and did not see their father's nakedness.
>
> Noah awoke from his wine and knew what his youngest son had done to him. He said, Cursed be Canaan, a slave of slaves will he be to his broth-ers. And he said, Blessed be the Lord, God of Shem, and Canaan will be a slave to him. May God enlarge Japheth, and he will dwell in the tents of Shem, and Canaan will be a slave to him. (9:18–27)

Let us recall the events in the Garden of Eden after the first Cre-ation (Genesis 2 and 3). God planted a garden and set the man in it to till it and tend it. In the garden were the Tree of Life and the Tree of the Knowledge of Good and Evil. Before eating the fruit of the Tree of Knowledge, the man and his wife were naked, but they were not ashamed. After eating the fruit, they covered themselves with cloth-ing and were subject to God's chastisement, which included a curse of the earth and the foretelling of the man's toil in earning his bread and of the subservience of the woman to the man.

The story of Noah's drunkenness is an inversion of the story of the Garden of Eden. The vine of Noah is a Tree of Ignorance. He drinks its wine and becomes drunk and then uncovers himself, reassum-ing the innocent nakedness of the first man and woman before their transgression. Ham, the son whose descendants will be cursed for his action—or inaction—does nothing to rectify his father's nakedness and simply tells his brothers what he has seen; he displays no sense of shame. Shem and Japheth, by contrast, understand that their father's state is not proper and cover him without looking upon his nakedness. When Noah awakens, he *knows* what Ham has done and curses his descendants with servitude to his brothers. The pattern is: fruit of a tree, loss of awareness, uncovering, lack of shame; and then, covering, knowledge, and a curse invoking servitude.

In addition to being another chapter in the reversal of the first Creation, this passage also continues the story of the second Creation that follows the Flood. The tree that is planted this time is a Tree of Ignorance—the loss of knowledge leads to the uncovering of nakedness. The question asked here is whether the reversal of the first Creation and the starting afresh with Noah extend even to the fundamental nature of humankind: Does the new beginning imply that human nature can revert to its original Edenic state? Does the new Creation begin with a slate that has been wiped completely clean?

The actions of Ham demonstrate the attitude of the peoples of Canaan (as well as the other descendants of Ham listed subsequently—in particular, the Egyptians) toward the question of human self-awareness. They show no shame, their attitude toward human nakedness—their knowledge of good and evil—is like that of the beasts of the field. Shem and Japheth, however, show the proper response to their father's nakedness: It is a temporary aberration that is not to be indulged. Noah, when he awakes, confirms this.

One of the functions of this description of the sons of Noah is to deliver a combined moral and political message, namely, that the behavior of the nations of Canaan—the peoples whom the Israelites supplant—is immoral and is not to be emulated, as is the behavior of the Egyptians, in whose land the Israelites dwelt previously. The viewpoint implied in the episode of Noah and the vineyard is that any putative return to a pre-moral state can only be disingenuous. Moral awareness is part of human nature and is not subject to change, no matter how radical a new beginning takes place.

Will Noah Die?

In the preceding chapter we interpreted the awareness gained by eating of the Tree of Knowledge as relating to corporeality and death, and we suggested that this awareness is part of the basis for a moral consciousness. If we pursue this approach to the knowledge of good and evil, then the story of Noah is also about the possibility of the loss of the knowledge of mortality that is a fundamental defining feature of human nature. The question then might be: Can the place of mortality in human nature change? Can we in fact become immortal once more, at least in the sense of no longer being subject to the awareness of death?

At the beginning of this chapter we pointed out a connection between Noah and his great-grandfather Enoch, the only descendant of Adam who is not subject to death. We saw there that both Enoch and Noah walked with God, and that both of their names play on the root ḤN, "favor." We are therefore now led to wonder whether Noah too, who escapes the common lot of the rest of humanity in the Flood, might not also escape the *final* common destiny of the rest of mankind. And in fact, the character who is saved from the Flood through divine favor in the parallel Near Eastern myths, Utnapishtim—as we saw in the preceding chapter—was granted immortality, thus completing the metaphor of escape from the general destiny.

The text itself poses this question in a subtle way, by the manner in which it presents the ancestry of Noah. The genealogy in Genesis 5 proceeds by repeating the following formula: "And X lived so-and-so many years and begot Y. And X lived so-and-so many years after begetting Y, and begot sons and daughters. And all the days of X were so-and-so many, and he died." This formula is repeated nine times, with the variations that we pointed out earlier in the cases of Enoch and Lemech, the father of Noah. When we get to Noah we read:

> Noah was five hundred years old and Noah begot Shem, Ham, and Japheth. And it was when men began to increase on the face of the earth
> . . . . (5:32–6:1)

The formula in the case of Noah is not completed, since the story of the Flood must be told before we can continue to Noah's ultimate fate. The preceding list presented us, again and again, with the refrain ". . . and he died," with which each short biography ends—a refrain that does not appear in any other genealogical list in the Pentateuch. The litany is interrupted first with the story of the deathless Enoch, and then with the life of Noah. With Noah, we are held in suspense until after the Flood, the covenant, and the vineyard episodes. Noah survives the Flood, escaping the death that befell all humanity. Noah's drunkenness and nakedness take him back, as we saw, to the Garden of Eden. And Noah "walked with God," just like his great-grandfather Enoch. So, will Noah be like Enoch, who "was not, for God took him"? The final answer to this question follows the vineyard episode, the seeming reversal of the eating from the Tree of Knowledge, the eating that resulted in true mortality:

> And Noah lived after the Flood for three hundred and fifty years. All the days of Noah were nine hundred and fifty years, and he died. (9:28–29)

Noah is not Utnapishtim. Human nature will not change.

The Consolation of Noah

The story of Noah and the vineyard carries associations in addition to the references to the themes of mortality and morality that we discussed above. Let us look once again at the explanation of Noah's name as given in the text:

> Lemech lived one hundred and eighty-two years and he begot a son. He called him Noah [NoaḤ] to say, This one will comfort us [YêNaḤaMeNu] from our works and from the toil of our hands from the earth which the Lord has cursed. (5:28–29)

What is the comfort or consolation that Noah is supposed to bring? The first idea that comes to mind is that Noah's survival of the Flood is a consolation to humanity, in the sense that the continuity of the human race is assured and that the human race has not reached its end.[1] But his naming speaks of comforting us from our deeds and our sad labors; this apparently refers not to survival of the species, but to consolation from some kind of suffering to which humans are subject that is connected with their toiling in the world.

The consolation that Noah brings has been proposed to come from his invention of wine, which "makes the heart of man joyous" (Psalms 104:15). Wine gives respite, however temporary, from the grim toil decreed for man on his expulsion from the Garden:

. . . may the earth be accursed on your account; with suffering will you eat of it all the days of your life. (3:17)

Wine offers consolation for the loss of the easy life that man had in the Garden before he ate the fruit of the Tree of Knowledge of Good and Evil. But wine also makes men forget, and lose inhibitions that were acquired as a result of eating the forbidden fruit—as in the case of Noah, who takes off his clothes. As Noah's story is part of the reversal of the original Creation, and as the vine—the Tree of Ignorance— is the reversed image of the Tree of Knowledge, drinking wine actually returns man to his original state of ignorance before eating the fruit offered by his wife. Although the drunkenness brought on by wine will not reverse human nature with regard to being subject to the knowledge of mortality, it can result in a transient forgetfulness of this sad knowledge. In this sense, then, Noah created an avenue for a return to the Garden, even if only for a few hours.

Rebuilding

The issue of mortality has now been closed forever, but the question of God's response to the corruption of His creatures arises once more in the later story of the cataclysm that overtakes Sodom and Gomorrah. God has decided to destroy the wicked cities, but in deference to Abraham, will permit his nephew Lot to escape. Two angels are sent to take Lot out of the city while there is still time; Lot feeds them and they prepare to stay the night:

> Before they went to sleep, the people of the city, the people of Sodom, gathered around the house from young man to old, all the people from the whole town. They called to Lot and said to him, Where are the men who came to you tonight? Bring them out to us so that we may know them. Lot went out to them to the entrance, and closed the door behind him and said, Please my brothers, do not do evil. Here I have two daughters who have not known a man, let me bring them out to you and do what you wish to them, only to these men do nothing, for they have come under the shelter of my roof. They said, Get out of the way! And they said, Someone who has moved here as an alien—he presumes to act as a judge? And now we will do even worse to you than to them; and they pressed the man Lot

greatly, and approached to break the door. The [two] men put out their hand and brought Lot in to them into the house and closed the door. And they struck with blindness the people who were at the entrance of the house, from small to great, and they were unable to find the entrance. (19:4–11)

The angels pull Lot and his wife and daughters from the town, God rains brimstone and fire on Sodom and the surrounding area, and Lot's wife makes the mistake of looking back and is turned into a pillar of salt. The death of Lot's wife—the result of her reluctance to leave Sodom behind—is necessary for what follows:

Lot went up from Ṣoar and stayed on the mountain and his two daughters with him, for he was afraid to stay in Ṣoar, and he stayed in a cave, he and his two daughters. The elder said to the younger, Our father is old, and there is no man in the land to cohabit with us in the way of all the land. Let us give our father wine to drink, and let us lie with him and cause seed to live from our father. They gave their father wine to drink on that night, and the elder came and lay with her father, and he did not know of her lying down and her arising. The next day, the elder said to the younger, I lay with my father last night; let us give him wine to drink tonight also, and come and lie with him, and we will cause seed to live from our father. They gave their father wine to drink on that night also, and the younger arose and lay with him, and he did not know of her lying down and her arising. The two daughters of Lot conceived by their father. The elder bore a son, and gave him the name Moab [from Me-AB, "of the father"]; he is the ancestor of the Moabites of today. The younger bore a son also, and gave him the name Ben-ami ["son of my kin"]; he is the ancestor of the Ammonites [BêNe ʿaMoN] of today. (19:30–38)

These passages connect to both the vineyard episode in the story of Noah and the Tree of Knowledge story. The stories of Noah and of Lot are parallel in the corruption of the inhabitants of the earth and of the cities and God's decision to destroy them, while preserving one man and his family. After the destruction, the survivor drinks wine, becomes intoxicated, and is subjected to an immoral action by his child or children. The descendants of the immoral children are the nations who will later be the major enemies of the Israelites: Egypt and Canaan the children of Ham, son of Noah, and Moab and Ammon, the products of the incestuous coupling of Lot and his daughters.[2]

84

We have already seen the affinities between the story of Noah's vineyard and the story of the Tree of Knowledge. Some of the same themes appear in the story of Lot. Thus, when the townspeople of Sodom converge on the house of Lot, they demand that his guests be brought out to them so that they may "know them"; Lot attempts to appease them by offering them his daughters "who have not known a man"; and the angels rescue Lot by striking the people blind. The demand for sexual "knowledge" is answered with blindness—an ironic reference to the Tree of Knowledge, whose fruit caused the eyes of the first man and his wife to be opened. The ironies are multiplied in the account of Lot and his daughters when the daughters, who have "not known a man," lose this status by lying with their father himself, the man whose moral obtuseness permitted him to offer his own daughters to the rampaging townsmen. And, of course, Lot is first intoxicated by drinking wine, so that "he did not know of her lying down and her arising." The "unknown" daughters are "known" by Lot himself, but only as a result of his ignorance of what he is doing. And the professed motive of the daughters is to secure the continuation of the human race by beginning to procreate after the devastation, to begin again, as Noah did after the Flood. The expression "to cause seed to live," had been used before in Noah's rescue of the animals in the ark (7:3). "Causing seed to live" alludes also to the "mother of all living beings," Eve, who was given this name after the first couple ate the fruit of the Tree of Knowledge.

Evasion of the knowledge of good and evil characterizes the enemies of the Israelites and thus justifies their being supplanted by them. The nations from whom the Israelites must remain separate are corrupt—they are vestiges of worlds that God has destroyed. Just as Ham is unable to rise above the corruption of the generation of the Flood, so too are the daughters of Lot true children of Sodom, as they are the children of their father's moral blindness.

Knowledge and Knowledge

The interplay among the different types of knowledge—the carnal, the moral, and the cognitive—is continued in other places in Genesis. The use of the verb "to know" in its sexual meaning is quite restricted in Genesis; it is used in this way in only six places. The first three mentions of this kind of knowledge are in connection with Adam and his family:

> The man knew Eve his wife and she conceived and bore Cain . . . . (4:1);

> Cain knew his wife and she conceived and bore Enoch . . . . (4:17);

> Adam knew his wife again, and she bore a son, and she named him Seth . . . . (4:25).

These "knowings" are the first beginnings of the human race.

Carnal knowledge is ironically associated with the man's initial lack of awareness.[3] In the Eden story the term is used immediately after the man is given the fruit of the Tree of Knowledge by the woman. The woman ate the fruit first, so the man had not yet attained this knowledge at the time that she gave him the fruit to eat. As soon as the knowledge is gained by both of them, they cover themselves, thus obscuring their knowledge. However, the man then "knew Eve his wife"—who was "bone of my bone and flesh of my flesh" (2:23)—and thereby comes to know his own flesh in its corporeality and its mortality.

Carnal knowledge is not mentioned through all the following generations, until we get to Lot and his daughters:

> Bring them out to us so that we may know them. Lot went out to them to the entrance, and closed the door behind him and said, Please my brothers, do not do evil. Here I have two daughters who have not known a man . . . . (19:5–8)

And then, after each time that he is seduced by one of his daughters:

> . . . and he did not know of her lying down and her arising. (19:33, 19:35)

We have already seen how the irony is played upon in the story of Lot and his daughters—who are also flesh of Lot's flesh, as Eve was flesh of Adam's flesh—as he sleeps with the daughters who have not known a man, but without knowing that he is doing so.

The next mention of knowledge in its metaphorical sense is in the account in Genesis 24 of the mission of Abraham's servant to find and bring home a wife for his master's son, Isaac. Abraham has sent the servant to Abraham's homeland to find a girl. When the servant reaches the well where the daughters of the families come to fetch water, he prays to the God of his master for a sign that will enable him to tell whether the girl he meets is the right one. He prays that when he asks one of the girls to give him some water to drink, the chosen one will of her own accord offer to draw water for his camels also. This is no small matter, since the text tells us that he has no fewer than ten camels with him, and camels are well known for their water capacity, especially after a journey:

> . . . by her will I know that You have done kindness with my master. Before he had done speaking, Rebecca came out, who had been born to Bethuel the son of Milka, the wife of Nahor, brother of Abraham, and her jug was on her shoulder. The girl was very beautiful, a virgin, and no man had known her . . . . (24:14–16)

The girl who appears first is none other than his master's great-niece, Rebecca, "a virgin, and no man had known her," including, of course (in the literal sense of the word), the servant himself. And not only does she allow him to drink from her jug, she even offers to water his camels. The servant, watching her, "wondered at her, silently, to know whether the Lord had made his mission succeed or not" (24:21). As we know, the Lord did. The unknown girl is herself the sign by which he knows.

However, there is more to it than this. As the servant and Rebecca approach the home of his master, the girl sees her future husband Isaac coming toward them and, on being told who he is, covers herself with a veil (24:65). We will see in detail in a later chapter how Rebecca thwarts her husband's wish to bless his older son by a daring deception: She has the younger Jacob cover himself with goatskins and wear his brother's clothing in order to mislead Isaac into giving Jacob the blessing that was intended for the firstborn Esau (Genesis 27). The woman whom "no man had known" covers herself, and her motives and her actions, from her husband.

A veil like Rebecca's reappears in the next and last instance of sexual knowledge, the episode of Judah and his daughter-in-law, Tamar, in Genesis 38. Tamar forces Judah to face a responsibility that he had been trying to avoid; her means of accomplishing this is to disguise herself with a veil, and thereby to deceive Judah into fathering her sons. There are affinities with the Lot story, as Tamar's stratagem is played out on the backdrop of a calamity that endangers her ability to bear a child. Her first husband has died without offspring; when his brother, Onan, takes his place as her husband, he refuses to impregnate her, for which God kills him too. The reason for the *coitus interruptus* of Onan is itself a play on the different senses of knowledge we have been discussing: "... for he knew that the seed would not be his." Onan's knowledge of the attribution of the seed motivates his refusal to "know" his brother's widow.

Tamar is told to wait for the third brother to grow up, but Judah does not fulfill his promise that she will be married to his youngest son. As was true for the daughters of Lot after the destruction of Sodom, all the men who could have given Tamar children have either been killed by God or are otherwise not available. Tamar, therefore, like the daughters of Lot, takes matters into her own hands and brings about her conception by deceiving, not her father, but her father-in-law, after the death of his wife. She takes off her widow's garments and covers herself with a veil:

> Judah saw her and thought she was a harlot, for she had covered her face. He went off to her to the road and said, Come let me lie with you; for he did not know that she was his daughter-in-law . . . Judah recognized [them] and said, She is more in the right than I, for I did not give her to my son Shela; and he did not know her again. (38:15–16, 38:26)

When Judah recognizes his responsibility for Tamar's pregnancy he acknowledges it, and "he did not know her again," as he had in fact not known her before, when he did "know" her. In all cases where a woman is described as not being known by a man, the meaning is at least double, and heavy with irony. These narratives play on both the Tree of Knowledge story and on other episodes that are themselves plays on the Tree of Knowledge story.

This discussion of knowledge in its several meanings illustrates a general principle in the interrelationships among the narratives in the Book of Genesis: A single story will often be connected to several other stories under different paradigms. Thus, while the story of Noah and the vineyard is related through the theme of mortality to the Garden of Eden episode, it is also part of the development of the themes of sexual immorality among the nations (Canaan, Egypt, Ammon, and Moab) and betrayal of a father by his children (Lot and his daughters, Isaac and Jacob). There is a related theme of the relationship between men and women that is taken up in the stories of Lot and his daughters, of Isaac and Rebecca, and of Judah and Tamar, which is also an outgrowth of the Tree of Knowledge episode; in this thread is incorporated the role of women in initiating the creation and preservation of life. In addition, there is the paradigm of the competition of the younger child with the older, in which the story of Rebecca and Jacob plays a part. This paradigm is introduced in the murder of Abel by Cain, and continues through the stories of Isaac and Ishmael, Jacob and Esau, Rachel and Leah, Joseph and his brothers, and Ephraim and Menashe, the sons of Joseph.

The paradigm of the manipulation of the unsuspecting man by the woman is developed through several stages. From Lot's daughters, whose immorality finds a parallel in the story of Noah and his sons, it is transformed into a part of the struggle between the younger and the older (Rebecca and Isaac, Jacob and Esau), an intersection with the stories of the competing brothers (or sisters), and finally becomes the woman's way—since she is often powerless to achieve her end in any other way—of forcing the man to fulfill his obligations (Tamar and Judah). A common denominator, as we saw, is that the woman acts in the perceived interests of her children, whether living or yet unborn, and that she relies on her resourcefulness to circumvent the constraints of male authority.

In later chapters we will discuss at greater length the paradigms that have their origin in the Tree of Knowledge story, paradigms involving knowledge and blindness, opening of the eyes, covering and clothing. We will see there how the progressive development of these paradigms expresses a central concern of the book—the development of the relationship between God and human beings.

Notes

1. One of the medieval Jewish commentators (Shmuel ben Meir, "Rashbam," eleventh-twelfth century) points out that Noah's birth followed the first natural death of a human being, the death of Adam. Noah's entering the world was thus a consolation that was sorely needed after mortality had actually been witnessed for the very first time by anyone, and the abstract knowledge of mortality that people had had earlier was now knowledge gained from experience.

2. Ammon and Moab continue to be associated with their incestuous origin later on. In Deuteronomy 23:3–4 we read: "No bastard shall come into the congregation of the Lord, even the tenth generation shall not come into the congregation of the Lord. No Ammonite or Moabite shall come into the congregation of the Lord, even the tenth generation shall not come into the congregation of the Lord, forever." In biblical usage, a bastard is one born of either an adulterous or an incestuous union, not simply the child of unmarried parents.

3. There may be another aspect common to all the uses of "to know" in its sexual sense—that it is the term used for a sexual relationship which is not socially sanctioned. In the case of Adam and Cain and their wives, the term is used not because these unions were illicit, but because at this early stage of humanity, the social structure that could give them legitimacy did not yet exist. There is nonetheless an intriguing hint of incest in these liaisons: Adam's wife is literally of his own flesh, while Cain's wife is perforce his sister. In the later instances the sexual relationship—always extramarital—is also sometimes incestuous (Lot and his daughters, Judah and Tamar).

PART TWO

Patriarchs and Progeny: Blind Fathers

CHAPTER 5

Abraham and Isaac:
Failure in Succession

THE THEMES OF CREATION AND THE ORIGINS AND
nature of humanity occupy the first eleven chapters of Genesis. Genesis 12 ushers in the story of the beginnings of the
nation of Israel, starting with the Patriarchs. God tells the first Patriarch, Abraham, to leave his homeland in Mesopotamia and travel to
the land of Canaan, where his descendants will become a great nation.
Abraham, his wife Sarah, and his nephew Lot arrive in Canaan where
God promises Abraham that this land will belong to his descendants.
Abraham and Sarah have no children as yet, although Abraham is
already 75 years old and Sarah is ten years younger. Abraham, as the
founder of a new cult that serves the Lord exclusively, builds altars
and worships God. But Abraham needs an heir to carry on what will
become a tradition. The stories of the three Patriarchs—Abraham,
Isaac, and Jacob—are largely concerned with the story of the vicissitudes of the transmission of Abraham's legacy.

After many years of childlessness—and after Abraham fathers a
son with Sarah's Egyptian handmaid—the mantle of the succession
ultimately rests on Isaac, the son finally born to Abraham and Sarah.
Although the question of an heir for Abraham is now apparently
resolved, the preservation and continuation of the tradition by Isaac
and his children do not turn out to be so simple. The trouble starts
with Isaac himself, whose name reflects a major problem in maintain-
ing a tradition. The name Isaac in Hebrew is YiṢHaQ, from the root
ṢHQ, meaning "to laugh."

The Disappointment of Isaac

To get some idea of the problems posed by the fact that Isaac is the one to continue the tradition begun by Abraham, we will need to run through a quick summary of the life of Isaac. The first mention of Isaac by name comes in Genesis 17:

> God said to Abraham, no longer call Sarai your wife by the name Sarai, for Sarah will be her name. I will bless her and I will give you a son of her ... And Abraham fell on his face and laughed [VaYiṢḤaQ], and he said to himself, Can a child be born to a hundred-year-old man? And Sarah— can a ninety-year-old woman give birth? So Abraham said to God, May Ishmael [Abraham's son by Sarah's handmaid] live before You. God said, But no, your wife Sarah will bear you a son, and you will call him Isaac [YiṢḤaQ] ... As for Ishmael, I have listened to you [ŠêM'aTiKa, a play on the root of Ishmael, ŠM']; I will bless him and I will make him fruitful and I will multiply him greatly ... But My covenant I will fulfill with Isaac .... (17:15–21)

Abraham's laughter expresses his incredulity. We will return later to the opposition that is here set up between the chosen son, Isaac, and Ishmael, the son of the handmaid Hagar.

The next mention of Isaac, and the accompanying laughter, appear when three supernatural visitors come to Abraham and Sarah and one of them foretells his birth:

> He said, I will return to you at this time next year and your wife Sarah will have a son; and Sarah was listening at the tent door, which was behind him. Now Abraham and Sarah were old, advanced in years, and Sarah had ceased to have women's periods. Sarah laughed [VaTiṢḤaQ] to herself and said, After I have withered will I become youthful again? And my husband is old as well. The Lord said to Abraham, Why did Sarah laugh [ṢaḤaQa] and say, Is it possible for me to bear a child now that I have grown old? Is anything too great for the Lord? At the appointed time I will return to you next year and Sarah will have a son. But Sarah denied it and said, I did not laugh [Lo ṢaḤaQTi], because she was afraid. And He said, No, you did laugh [ṢaḤaQT]. (18:10–15)

Abraham's incredulousness is here joined by Sarah's, but with an admixture of the ridiculous in the odd argument about whether or not Sarah had really laughed. Sarah's denial of her laughter makes it clear that it was not a smile of delight of which she stood accused, but rather a mocking—perhaps bitter—laugh. Clearly she has no faith in what the stranger predicts.

Laughter appears again in Genesis 21, at the time of the birth of Isaac:

> Abraham was one hundred years old when his son Isaac was born to him. Sarah said, God has made sport [ṢêḤoQ] with me, everyone who hears will laugh [YiṢḤaQ] because of me. And she said, Who would say to Abraham that Sarah would nurse children? And now I have borne a son for his old age! (21:5–7)

We hear nothing more about Isaac until we come to the famous story of his near-sacrifice by his father at God's command (Genesis 22). God tests Abraham by telling him to take his son Isaac and sacrifice him on a mountain that God will reveal later. Abraham takes Isaac, together with everything he needs for the sacrifice—wood, knife, fire—to the mountain. On the way up the mountain Isaac asks his father where the sacrificial lamb is and says nothing in reply to Abraham's evasive answer—"The Lord will see to the lamb for the sacrifice" (22:8). Abraham binds Isaac and raises the knife to kill him when he is stopped at the last minute by a voice from heaven: "Do not raise your hand against the boy and do not do anything to him, for now I know that you fear God, that you did not withhold your only son from Me" (22:12). After the ordeal they return together to their home in Beersheba.

Some time later, Abraham sends his servant to his homeland in Mesopotamia to bring back a girl for Isaac to marry. The servant travels to the homeland of Abraham and, after asking for a sign that will enable him to identify the right girl, is met by Rebecca, the granddaughter of Abraham's brother. He takes her back to Canaan and Isaac marries her (Genesis 24).

Rebecca conceives and bears twins. The boys are as different as can be right from the start: Esau, the firstborn, is ruddy and hairy, while his brother Jacob is smooth-skinned. Esau becomes a skilled hunter, a man of the field, while Jacob is described as a tent-dweller, one who stays at home. Esau is Isaac's favorite, while Rebecca loves Jacob (Genesis 25). When Isaac gets old and his eyesight fails, he tries to bestow a blessing on Esau, but Rebecca and Jacob take advantage of Isaac's blindness to trick him into blessing Jacob instead (Genesis 27).

Before the story of Isaac's deception by his wife and younger son, we read of two episodes in the life of Isaac that tell us something about Isaac's persona, especially by implicitly comparing him to his father, Abraham. Isaac and Rebecca move temporarily to Gerar, the land ruled by the Philistine king, Abimelech (Genesis 26). The root ṢḤQ reappears here, now for the last time in the story of Isaac, in the context of an embarrassing mishap concerning Isaac and his wife. In order to understand the import of this part of Isaac's story it will first be necessary to summarize the similar events in the life of Abraham.

In Genesis 20 we are told that Abraham and his wife had also settled for a time in Gerar, where Abraham had given the inhabitants to understand that his wife Sarah was in reality his sister. Assuming that Sarah was an unmarried woman, the king, also called Abimelech, had her brought to his palace and kept her there overnight. God appeared to him in a dream and warned him that Sarah was a married woman and that her husband Abraham was a prophet, and that if he did not restore her to her husband forthwith, he and everyone in his household would die. Abimelech summoned all his servants in the morning and told them his dream, and they were filled with fear. He then returned Sarah to Abraham, together with gifts of cattle and slaves, and offered him the choice of his land to dwell in.

In Genesis 21 we read of a dispute between Abraham and Abimelech over the ownership of a well. Abraham confronts the king with the fact that Abimelech's servants had stolen a well from him. The king makes excuses. The two then solemnize a pact, and Abraham gives Abimelech in addition seven sheep that will serve as an affirmation that Abraham had indeed dug the well.

There are similar accounts concerning Isaac's wife and conflicts over wells in the story of Isaac and Abimelech in Genesis 26, but the interactions between Abimelech and Isaac are very different from those between Abimelech and Abraham. Isaac, like Abraham, starts out by telling the people of Gerar that his wife is his sister, but then the story diverges from that of Abraham and Sarah. Abimelech does not take Rebecca to his palace, as happened with Sarah; on the contrary, she remains with Isaac. Then Rebecca's true status is revealed in a way that leaves no room for doubt:

> When he [Isaac] had been there for a long time, Abimelech the king of the Philistines looked through the window and saw Isaac sporting [MêṢaḤeQ] with his wife Rebecca. Abimelech summoned Isaac and said, So she is really your wife! Why did you say "She is my sister?" . . . One of the people almost lay with your wife! (26:8–10)

It is not the king who almost sins with his wife, but only "one of the people," suggesting that perhaps Isaac's wife is not special enough to merit the king's attention. Isaac and Rebecca's discovery by Abimelech peering in at the window and observing them "sporting" is undignified—even comical—and very different from the manner in which the earlier Abimelech learned that Sarah was actually Abraham's wife.

Isaac acquires great wealth in Gerar, and the people begin to envy him. As a result, Abimelech sends him away unceremoniously: "Go from us, for you have become too great for us" (26:16). Isaac then leaves Gerar. He settles nearby and starts to redig the wells that his father had dug:

> Isaac dug once again the wells that they had dug in the time of his father Abraham, which the Philistines had stopped up after Abraham's death, and he called them the same names that his father had called them. (26:18)

Note that the Philistines would not have dared to stop up the wells when Abraham was still alive, but once he is dead they show no comparable awe of Isaac. When Isaac's servants dig and find water, the Philistines claim the water as their own. In the disputes over wells between Isaac's shepherds and the shepherds of Gerar, there are no dramatic confrontations in which Isaac rebukes the Philistines and they excuse themselves, as had happened between Abraham and Abimelech. Isaac simply remains silent and has his servants keep on digging wells until the Philistines leave them alone.

Isaac cannot escape his name. His treatment by Abimelech and the people of Gerar lacks the seriousness and the respect that were accorded Abraham in similar circumstances. Isaac is a copy of Abraham, but a much diminished copy.

Isaac's portrayal as a none-too-successful follower of Abraham is reinforced by what God tells Isaac on the two occasions that He speaks to him. God blesses Isaac not because of Isaac's merits, but because of Abraham's:

> The Lord appeared to him and said, Do not go down to Egypt; dwell in the land that I tell you. Live in this land and I will be with you and I will bless you, for I will give all these lands to you and to your children, and I will fulfill the oath that I swore to Abraham your father. I will multiply your offspring like the stars of the sky, and I will give to your offspring all of these lands, and all the nations of the earth will bless themselves by your offspring, because Abraham heeded Me and kept My charge and My commandments, My statutes and My laws. (26:2–5)

And similarly in the second theophany:

> The Lord appeared to him on that night and said, I am the God of your father Abraham; do not be afraid, for I am with you and I will bless you and I will multiply your offspring for the sake of My servant Abraham. (26:24)

In this way too, Isaac appears as a weak echo of Abraham.

The rest of Isaac's story is consistent with his portrayal as a character with little importance on his own account. Isaac's is a purely passive persona: His fate is determined by the actions of others, and in those cases where he himself acts, he usually does no more than imitate the actions of his father. Abraham, in visiting the land of Abimelech, called his wife his sister, and Isaac in the same situation does the same; when Isaac digs wells, they are rediggings of the very same wells that Abraham had dug before him, and Isaac gives them the same names that Abraham did.

The root for "laughter" that underlies Isaac's name and that appears repeatedly in his story signifies more than one kind of mirth. At first, Abraham and Sarah betray by their laughter their incredulity at ever having a child. When Isaac is finally born, Sarah says:

> ... God has made sport [ṢêḤoQ] with me, everyone who hears will laugh [YiṢḤaQ] because of me. And she said, Who would say to Abraham that Sarah would nurse children? And now I have borne a son for his old age! (21:6–7)

The laughter here can have several meanings, and in fact has been translated and understood in different ways by various interpreters. This laughter can signify joy and rejoicing, so that Sarah could be saying, "God has brought me laughter; everyone who hears will rejoice with me (or for me)." A second possible translation is "God has made sport with me, everyone who hears will laugh at me," where the incongruity of an old woman nursing a baby might elicit ridicule and mockery. I have chosen to translate the text in a way that allows for any of several interpretations: "Everyone who hears will laugh because of me" can have either of the two meanings mentioned here, as well as a third meaning—that people will laugh in surprise and wonder at the report of an event whose occurrence could never have been contemplated.

One aspect of the different meanings is that what is being promised or reported is not taken seriously—and lack of seriousness, above all, is what characterizes the story of Isaac. But more precisely, what all the types of laughter share in the story of Isaac is the sense of the overturning of expectations—a sense of playing or sporting, which can take the form of laughter at a pleasant surprise or, at the other extreme, of a sneer signifying sarcasm or mockery.

The story of Isaac is replete with instances of things happening against all expectations, with surprises both pleasant and unpleasant. The promise to Abraham and Sarah that they will have a child flies in the face of the fact of their advanced age. The actual birth of Isaac is a retort to their lack of faith in God's promise. Once Isaac is a reality and it appears possible that Abraham's descendants will indeed be as numerous as the stars—as God has promised—God tells Abraham to kill his son. Then, when Abraham attempts to obey God's command to sacrifice his son—having accepted God's decree that Isaac should die—God tells him *not* to kill him. And the most important overturning of expectations is the disappointment that is implicit in the feeble character of Isaac, who was supposed to be the one to pass the banner of Abraham on to future generations. Isaac may repeat the actions of Abraham, but he is clearly no Abraham.

The Sacrifice of Isaac

What in the story of Isaac might account for his passivity and his blindness, and for his failure to elicit the respect that Abraham commanded? And what effect does Isaac's personality—or his lack of personality—have on the following generations? We will suggest an answer to the first question before going on to deal with the second.

Isaac is a shadow of his father, as we saw from his repetition of the actions of Abraham in his dealings with Abimelech. Nonetheless, his status as the son of Abraham is enough for him to merit God's special consideration. He is the fulfillment of God's promise to his father and is to be the channel through which the tradition of Abraham will be transmitted. In all these ways Isaac is portrayed as secondary to Abraham and as having no independent life of his own.

The pivotal event in Isaac's life is his father's attempt to sacrifice him in order to carry out God's command. Isaac's character as an instrument is defined in this episode: He is an instrument that Abraham uses to demonstrate his obedience to God. Isaac is thus a sacrifice in a deeper sense than we might understand from the story of his binding and near-slaughter by his father—Isaac is not only offered up as a sacrifice *by* Abraham; he is at the same time a sacrifice *to* Abraham.[1,2] In this way he is a victim of the fate common to many sons of great men, an overshadowing and stunting like that of a plant growing in the shade of a great tree.

Isaac is certainly overshadowed by his father, but he is more than simply overshadowed—if the angel had not intervened, Abraham would have killed him to show his devotion to God. We can speculate about the effect that such an experience might have had on a young boy. Perhaps Isaac's stunted personality can be traced back to the devastating realization that his father was about to slaughter him like a sacrificial animal. And further, perhaps Isaac's blindness is meant to suggest that the enormity of this experience rendered him incapable of perceiving what was in front of his eyes, that only by repressing this horrible truth could he carry on at all.

In introducing the story of Isaac's attempt to bless Esau and the thwarting of this attempt by the subterfuge carried out by Rebecca and Jacob, the text tells us that Isaac had become blind in his old age

(27:1). An early Midrashic treatment of this verse (Genesis Rabba 65:10) explains how Isaac's blindness had its origin in his near-slaughter by his father: When Isaac was lying bound, waiting for the knife-stroke, the angels looked down from heaven and wept; their tears fell into Isaac's eyes and left traces that caused him to become blind when he grew old. Perhaps this Midrash is hinting that the angels inadvertently protected Isaac from realizing what was happening to him by predisposing him to blindness.

Whether or not these speculations about the origin of Isaac's blindness reflect the intent of the text, the story in Genesis appears to be suggesting that Isaac's was not a blindness of the eyes alone. Of his two sons, Isaac favors Esau, the hunter, over Jacob, the stay-at-home, and wishes to bestow a blessing on Esau despite the fact that he is clearly not suited to carry on the tradition of Abraham. For besides being a hunter and man of the fields, Esau marries local Canaanite girls, to the chagrin of both his parents. Intermarriage with the daughters of the land carries with it the danger of assimilation into the local milieu and the consequent loss of Abraham's unique tradition. The same Esau had also earlier sold his birthright—which he "scorned"—for a meal of lentil stew (Genesis 25). Isaac must have been blind indeed if he could not see that Esau was unworthy.

An alternative, admittedly speculative, possibility for Isaac's preferring Esau brings us back again to Isaac's trauma at the hands of his father: Perhaps Isaac chose Esau over Jacob precisely because Esau was the son who resembled Abraham the least. In other words, perhaps Isaac's attempt to bless Esau was a covert rebellion against the father who tried to slaughter him.

These speculations propose that it is his father's actions that are ultimately to blame for Isaac's lack of *gravitas*. Let us turn now to the repercussions that Isaac's shortcomings have on *his* sons, the second question that we posed above.

Isaac was a copy, however attenuated, of his father Abraham. Who are the models for Jacob and Esau, sons of an absent father? How do they become the men they are, if their father is indeed as feeble as Isaac appears to be?

Esau at first takes no model at all; he reverts to the field as a primitive hunter and is susceptible to assimilation into the culture of the

Canaanites. It is characteristic that his response to his parents' disappointment at his taking Hittite wives is to marry a daughter of his uncle Ishmael, who makes his living in the wilderness as an archer (21:20), and who is described as "a wild ass of a man, his hand raised against everyone, and everyone's hand raised against him" (16:12).

And Jacob? "Jacob was a simple man, a homebody" (25:27). He is the brother who stays at home and cooks lentil stew. The salient personality in his life is his mother, Rebecca, who initiates the scheme by which Isaac is deceived into thinking that he is blessing Esau when he is really blessing the disguised Jacob. Esau, wild and untrammeled, is the favorite of Isaac, while Jacob is the favorite of Rebecca (25:28). As we will see in the next chapter, Jacob will have to return to Abraham's homeland and start over in order to rid himself of the negative traits that he has inherited from his mother's family. The fatherless Jacob must be remade, acting in effect as his own father, while Esau, insofar as he finds a father at all, finds him in Ishmael—the violent son and husband of Egyptian women, the wild ass of a man who is no more than a model of the unrestrained man of the fields that Esau already is.

Abraham's Failed Heirs

There are two more appearances of the root for "laughter" in the story of Abraham, both of which have reference to the question of who will succeed Abraham and both of which signal the disappointment of expectations.

When Abraham first comes into the land of Canaan, he is accompanied by his wife Sarah and his nephew Lot, the son of his dead brother (12:4–5). Since at this time Abraham and Sarah had no son of their own, and since they were both quite old, Lot might have appeared to be the most likely candidate to be Abraham's heir. But Lot is disqualified. The root ṢḤQ is used in the story of Lot to hint at why he is eliminated from the running.

Lot parted from Abraham soon after their arrival in Canaan (Genesis 13) and chose to settle in Sodom. The chapter that immediately follows the annunciation of Isaac's birth contains the account of the destruction of the wicked cities of Sodom and Gomorrah, including the rescue of Lot by two of the same angels who had lately been visiting Abraham (Genesis 19).

When the angels, who have become Lot's guests, are threatened by the townspeople, Lot tries to protect them—but his plea to the citizens of Sodom is ignored and the rampaging townsmen try to break down the door. The angels rescue Lot and tell him to gather his family and to flee the impending cataclysm that will destroy the city. But once again he is ignored, this time by his own family:

> Lot went out and spoke to his sons-in-law, the husbands of his daughters, and said, Get up and leave this place, because the Lord is destroying the city—but his sons-in-law regarded him as though he were jesting [KiMêṢaḤeQ]. (19:14)

The root for "laughter" here signifies joking, and indicates the contempt with which Lot's sons-in-law greet his urgent plea.

Lot has no influence on those around him. Unlike Abraham, who is able to motivate others—his wife and his servant—to help him prepare a meal for the three angels who visit him (18:6–7), Lot can rely only on himself to make the guests feel welcome; no member of his household joins him in his hospitality.[3] When he tries to save his guests from being molested by his townsmen, his remonstrations are met with sarcasm and hostility:

> They said, Get out of the way! And they said, Someone who has moved here as an alien—he presumes to act as a judge? And now we will do even worse to you than to them . . . . (19:9)

And as we just saw, even his sons-in-law treat him with contempt. It is Lot's isolation that makes it impossible for him to be the bearer of the legacy of Abraham, as will soon become clear.

The second relevant occurrence of the root for "laughter" comes three verses after Isaac's birth and Sarah's speech about "everyone who hears will laugh because of me":

> Sarah saw the son of Hagar the Egyptian woman whom she had borne to Abraham sporting [or "playing" or "mocking"; MêṢaḤeQ]. She said to Abraham, Drive out this maidservant and her son, for the son of this maidservant will not inherit together with my son, with Isaac. (21:9–10)

After the laughter at Isaac's birth, Sarah's observation of Ishmael's "sporting" spurs her to have him expelled from her household. Although it is not clear what exactly it was in Ishmael's actions that precipitated Sarah's demand that he be sent away, the language that expresses his action—MêṢaHeQ, an oblique reference to Isaac (and the same word that described Lot)—as well as Sarah's assertion that he will not share in Isaac's inheritance, point to her real concern: Sarah is worried that Ishmael will compete with Isaac—will play the role of an Isaac—and may even come to supplant him. Sarah's fear that Ishmael will usurp Isaac's place can be laid to rest, for Ishmael will remain, like Lot, simply another failed heir for Abraham.

The text uses the same word—from the same root as Isaac's name—with reference to Isaac's two potential competitors for the role of Abraham's heir, Lot and Ishmael. A MêṢaHeQ is someone who plays, or mocks, or jests. This word would make a careful reader think of Isaac, and also of the association of Isaac with the lack of seriousness that is implicit in his name. Each of the competitors is deemed unworthy, and the association with the root for "laughter," ṢHQ, in each case signals this failure.

But why specifically are Lot and Ishmael disqualified? In order to answer this question we need to know what it is that is required of the heir of Abraham.

Before God carries out His intention to destroy Sodom, He says to Himself:

> . . . Will I hide from Abraham what I am doing? And Abraham will become a great and mighty nation, and all the nations of the earth will bless themselves by him. For I have known him, that he will command his children and his household after him, and they will keep the way of the Lord to do righteousness and justice . . . . (18:17–19)

Transmitting "the way of the Lord" to future generations by "commanding" those around him—it is because Abraham will do this that God values him. In contrast, Lot, singled out for rescue from the cataclysm of Sodom and Gomorrah because of his relationship to Abraham, has no influence on his townspeople, or even on his own family. We discussed Lot's isolation earlier, but another indication of his

Abraham and Isaac: Failure in Succession

inability to transmit the values of Abraham is evident in the story of what happens after the cataclysm. As we saw in our preceding chapter, Lot and his two unmarried daughters find refuge in a cave where the young women ply him with wine until he goes into a stupor, and then sleep with him in order to bear children (19:30–38). The products of these couplings are the ancestors of the nations of Moab and Ammon. Whatever their motives, Lot's daughters are children of Sodom more than they are products of a legacy transmitted through their father from Abraham.[4]

Ishmael, the next heir-apparent, is a biological son of Abraham, but he too will not be the chosen successor. After the maidservant Hagar and her son Ishmael are driven away at Sarah's insistence, Hagar finds Ishmael an Egyptian wife (21:21). The significance of this marriage becomes clear when we observe the great lengths to which Abraham goes in order to find a wife from his homeland for Isaac in order to ensure that the family will maintain its separateness from their idolatrous neighbors (Genesis 24). The description of Ishmael as a "wild ass of a man, his hand raised against everyone and everyone's hand raised against him" (Genesis 16) indicates how he influences those around him. He lives in the desert and becomes an expert bowman (Genesis 21). Although he too will be the father of a great nation, because he too is of the seed of Abraham, he is clearly no spiritual son of Abraham who can be counted on to carry his message to future generations.

But this brings us back to Isaac. Is Isaac really that different from Lot and Ishmael in the ways that count the most? Remember that when Abimelech spied on Isaac and Rebecca through the window, the verb that described Isaac's "sporting" was also MêṢaḤeQ—just like the others. Lot and Ishmael cannot be relied upon to continue the tradition of Abraham because of their inability to transmit this way of life to others, and especially to their children. Judged by this criterion, Isaac does no better than Lot or Ishmael. In fact, the disrespect with which Isaac is treated by Abimelech and the Philistines, Isaac's redigging of Abraham's wells—which he then calls by the same names that Abraham had given them—and his deception by his wife and son are practically echoes, respectively, of Lot's treatment by his

105

fellow townsmen and sons-in-law, his attempted emulation of Abraham's hospitality, and his passive manipulation by his daughters in the cave.

As we have already seen, Isaac's failure appears in his lack of impact on his sons, Jacob and Esau. We will discuss the story of Jacob and Esau in detail in the next chapter, and so I will give here only an abbreviated account that sheds light on the role of Isaac.

Isaac's older son, Esau, is a hunter and a man of the outdoors. He sells his birthright for the lentil stew that Jacob cooks—"Esau scorned the birthright" (25:34). He marries Hittite women, daughters of the land, thereby ensuring his assimilation into the surrounding culture (26:34–35). And later on, when Esau learns that his parents are upset about his taking local girls and therefore try to make sure that Jacob marries someone from the family of Abraham, he compounds his mistake by marrying a daughter of Ishmael, the "wild ass of a man" (28:9). In short, there is nothing in what we are told about Esau that would lead us to expect that he will continue the tradition of Abraham.

Unfortunately, what we read about Jacob is also not very encouraging. In addition to some fraternal extortion that he perpetrates on his own initiative in order to secure Esau's birthright (Genesis 25), he allows himself to be persuaded by his mother to deceive Isaac into bestowing on him a blessing intended for Esau (Genesis 27). His mother disguises him as Esau for this purpose, and Jacob unhesitatingly lies to his blind father and tells him that he is really Esau in order to obtain the blessing. The upshot of the story is that Jacob must begin all over again in a foreign land—like Abraham before him—in order to earn a blessing of his own. Only after Jacob reforms can he return to Canaan and take on the role of the next Patriarch.

Isaac's direct influence in the formation of both his sons is marginal. What we are left with in the end is the conclusion that, like Lot and Ishmael, Isaac too is in an important sense a failed heir of Abraham. Isaac's failure is already hinted at in his name, which foreshadows the lack of seriousness with which he will be regarded by those with whom he interacts.

Nevertheless—in spite of this failure—Isaac is still an instrument in the transmission of Abraham's legacy. By sending his son Jacob to

Abraham's homeland to find a wife, Isaac maintains his father's insistence that the family remain distinct from its immediate neighbors. Without this insistence, future generations will become Moabites or Ammonites, like the children of Lot; or Ishmaelites, like the children of Ishmael; or Edomites, like the children of Esau. In this way, Isaac's faithful copying of Abraham keeps the tradition in a state of suspended animation from which it can be revived in the next generation. The tortuous path taken by the further transmission of the legacy is described in our next chapter, in the story of Jacob.

Notes

1. Donna Avedisian suggested that Isaac can be seen as a sacrifice to Abraham.

2. Perhaps the two puzzling stories of Abraham's misrepresentation of his wife as his sister (in Egypt with Pharaoh in Genesis 12, and then with Abimelech in Gerar in Genesis 20) are further examples of Abraham's sacrificing the people closest to him, as he sacrifices both Isaac and, in a different way, his other son, Ishmael (Genesis 21).

3. The contrast between Lot and Abraham in their influence on others was pointed out by David Silber.

4. Lot's name, too, is played upon in the story of Lot by the fivefold repetition of words from the root MLT—"to escape, seek refuge"—in 19:17–22 and perhaps with the root PLT (also meaning "to escape") in 14:13.

CHAPTER 6

Jacob: Grasping the Heel,
Braving the Face

W E COME NOW TO THE THIRD OF THE PATRIARCHS, Jacob, who under his new name, Israel, becomes the father of the nation that will be known as the Children of Israel. The story of Jacob, like the story of Isaac, is also a story of what a son's character owes to his progenitors, and how the actions of that son, in turn, reverberate through the lives of his children. We will see how the narrative, in subtle ways, delivers a judgment on Jacob's actions by showing how Jacob's experiences reflect the consequences of those actions. And we will see how Jacob's deeds lead ultimately to his regeneration—but only with the aid of some divine nudgings hidden in his treatment by his mother's brother, in combination with some more readily apprehended appearances of a "*deus ex machina,*" as will become apparent.

Distance between the divine and the human is among the most important problems to be raised in the Book of Genesis, and a major issue in the later narratives of the Patriarchs is how they respond to this distance. In particular, we will see how the question of knowledge or ignorance of God's role in human affairs becomes more and more acute as the gulf widens.

Ignorance becomes a reigning motif with the story of Jacob, whose actions lay the groundwork in more than one way for the tortured relations among his sons. The early actions of Jacob represent one response to God's progressive concealment from human beings. In contrast to his grandfather Abraham, who obediently follows God's instructions, and to his father Isaac, who as we saw in the preceding chapter initiates nothing new, Jacob attempts repeatedly to force the hand of fate by straining to wrest from his older brother Esau his birthright and his blessing. Ignorant of what God has in store for him, Jacob tries, by hook or by crook, to achieve the status that an accident of fate has denied him. His unscrupulous efforts to gain for himself what he thinks he ought to have entail his long expiation at the hands of his uncle, and are echoed in the bitter rivalry among his own sons.

Jacob eventually comes to learn that by attempting to enhance his stature by illegitimate means he can only be diminished. As a result of his twenty-year ordeal with his uncle Laban in Haran, he is transformed from a schemer of oblique and devious means who steals his brother's blessing by deceit into a man who has earned his own blessing and is then capable of confronting his adversaries face to face.

The text uses a number of literary devices to reinforce different aspects of the narrative. First, the story of Jacob's expiation has a nested structure that expresses a correspondingly circular process in Jacob's development. Next is the sometimes ironic introduction of various symbolic objects—clothing, goats, stones—to sharpen our perception of the significance of the parts of the story by interrelating different episodes. In addition, the account is shaped by a set of three binary oppositions that define both the actions of Jacob and his character. The three axes determined by these oppositions are: wrong and expiation, conveyed through a color symbolism that is taken up in later prophetic and rabbinic literature; obliquity and following from behind—opposed to directness and confrontation—conveyed by means of an imagery of body parts; and the related opposition between crookedness and straightness, conveyed by means of word play. Finally, some of the key concepts involved in the growth and transformation of Jacob are presented in a progressive series of plays on Jacob's name, much as the development of the relations among Joseph and his brothers—as we will see in our next chapter—is portrayed in a series of verbal plays based on terms for recognition and estrangement.

Birthright and Blessing, and Poetic Justice

Let us begin with the introduction to the story of Jacob and Esau:

> These are the generations of Isaac the son of Abraham, Abraham begot
> Isaac. Isaac was forty years old when he took as a wife Rebecca the
> daughter of Bethuel the Aramean from Padan Aram, sister of Laban the
> Aramean. Isaac prayed to the Lord for his wife, for she was barren, and
> the Lord heeded his prayer, and Rebecca his wife conceived. The boys
> thrashed about within her and she said, If it be so, why am I like this?
> [meaning uncertain], and she went to inquire of the Lord. The Lord said
> to her, Two peoples are in your belly, and two nations will separate from
> your body; one nation will prevail over the other, and the older will serve
> the younger. Her time came to give birth, and there were twins in her
> belly. The first emerged ruddy, his whole body like a cloak of hair, and
> they named him Esau. His brother emerged afterward with his hand
> grasping Esau's heel ['eQeB], and he named him Jacob [Ya'aQoB] . . . .
> (25:19–26)

This narration of Rebecca's pregnancy and the birth of the twins
introduces some of the important symbols and motifs whose interplay will express the conflict between the two brothers and Jacob's
final successful emergence from the conflict. Let us simply note at
this time what those elements are before we see how they are or-
chestrated in the subsequent story of Jacob. First, we are told that
the boys' mother, Rebecca, is the sister of Laban the Aramean from
Padan Aram. The significance of this identification will become apparent when we see the roles that Rebecca and Laban play in the life
and development of Jacob, as will the import of the place of origin
of Rebecca's family. The struggle between the two sons in the womb
prefigures their struggle in later life, as the oracular reply to Rebecca's inquiry already indicates. Esau's ruddiness and hairiness are important for what follows, and the naming of Jacob (Ya'aQoB) (understood as meaning "he follows") with reference to the heel ('eQeB)
that he grasps will also be taken up later. Significant symbols and verbal elements that will be used include redness (of Esau) and white-
ness (the name LaBaN means "white"), and the heel ('eQeB), with its
connotations of deception and crookedness (another meaning of the
root 'QB is "crooked").

After this introduction we have the next encounter in the contest between the brothers:

> The boys grew up, and Esau became a skilled hunter, a man of the field, while Jacob was a simple man, a homebody [lit. "tent-dweller"]. Isaac loved Esau because he gave him game to eat, while Rebecca loved Jacob. Once Jacob made a stew and Esau came in from the field famished. Esau said to Jacob, Give me some of this red, red stuff [HaADoM HaADoM] to swallow because I'm famished, and this is why he is called Edom ["red"]. Jacob said, Sell me your birthright now. Esau said, I'm going to die anyway, so what good to me is a birthright? Said Jacob, Swear to me now. So he swore to him and sold his birthright to Jacob. Jacob gave Esau bread and lentil stew, and he ate and drank and got up and left, and Esau scorned the birthright. (25:27–34)

The feral nature of Esau that was hinted at in his redness and hairiness at birth is borne out in his later development, as he matures into a hunter, a man of the field, while Jacob is described as a tent-dweller. The natural contrast between the brothers is exacerbated by their father's favoring of the elder while their mother Rebecca favors the younger. In the episode that is narrated here, Jacob takes advantage of Esau's hunger and withholds food until Esau relinquishes the birthright. It is clear that the birthright means little to Esau ("Esau scorned the birthright"), but Jacob's preying on his brother's weakness to extort it from him is nonetheless not admirable. Redness is introduced once again with reference to Esau, this time as the color of the food that he hungrily demands from Jacob, in return for which he sells his birthright.

The next encounter between the brothers incorporates some of the same elements as the earlier one at the same time as it serves as the proximal trigger for the further adventures of Jacob. A long quote is preferable to an extensive paraphrase here:

> Esau was forty years old and he took as a wife Judith the daughter of Beeri the Hittite and Basmat the daughter of Elon the Hittite; and they were a source of bitterness for Isaac and Rebecca.
>
> When Isaac grew old and his eyes were too dim to see, he called Esau his elder son and said to him, My son, and he said to him, Here I am. And he said, I have grown old and I may die any day now. Now, take your weapons, your quiver and your bow, and go out into the field and hunt me

some game. And prepare for me the kind of delicacies that I like and bring them to me and I will eat so that I may bless you before I die.

Rebecca was listening when Isaac spoke to his son Esau. Esau went out to the field to hunt for game to bring in. Rebecca said to her son Jacob, I heard your father speaking to your brother Esau and he said, Bring me game and prepare for me delicacies and I will eat, and I will bless you before the Lord before I die. And now my son, listen to me, to what I charge you. Go to the flocks and take for me from there two choice goat-kids, and I will make delicacies of them for your father the way he likes. Bring them to your father and let him eat, so that he may bless you before he dies. Jacob said to Rebecca his mother, But my brother Esau is a hairy man, while I am a smooth man. Perhaps my father will feel me and he will think me a trickster, and I will bring on myself a curse and not a blessing. His mother said to him, Let your curse fall on me, my son; just listen to me and go get them for me.

So he went and got them and brought them to his mother, and his mother prepared delicacies such as his father liked. Rebecca took the good clothes of Esau her elder son that she had with her in the house, and she dressed her younger son Jacob in them. She covered his arms and the smooth part of his throat with the skins of the goat-kids. And she gave the delicacies and the bread that she had made to her son Jacob.

He came to his father and he said, Father, and he said, Yes; who are you, my son? Jacob said to his father, I am Esau your firstborn; I have done what you told me; arise and sit and eat of my game so that you may bless me. Isaac said to his son, How is it that you found it so quickly, my son? And he said, Because the Lord your God granted me good luck.

Then Isaac said to Jacob, Come near and let me feel you, my son—are you my son Esau or not? Jacob came near to his father Isaac and he felt him, and he said, The voice is the voice of Jacob but the arms are the arms of Esau. He did not recognize him because his arms were hairy like the arms of his brother Esau, and he blessed him. He said, Are you my son Esau? And he said, I am. So he said, Serve me and I will eat of my son's game so that I may bless you, and he served him and he ate, and he brought him wine and he drank. Then his father Isaac said to him, Come near and kiss me, my son. He came near and kissed him and he smelled the scent of his clothes and blessed him . . . . [Isaac then gives Jacob the blessing.]

When Isaac had done blessing Jacob and Jacob had just left his father Isaac, his brother Esau came in from his hunt. He too prepared delicacies and brought them to his father, and he said to his father, Let my father arise and eat of his son's game so that you may bless me. His father Isaac said to him, Who are you? And he said, I am your firstborn son Esau. Isaac was seized with a great trembling, and he said, Who then was it who hunted game and brought it to me and I ate of it all before you came and I blessed him? He will remain blessed.

When Esau heard his father's words he gave a great and a bitter cry, and he said to his father, Bless me too, Father! He said, Your brother came deceitfully [BêMiRMa] and took your blessing. And he said, He is indeed called Jacob [Ya'aQoB]; he has tricked me [VaYa'aQBeNi] now twice—he took my birthright [BêKoRaTi] and now he has taken my blessing [BiRKaTi]. And he said, But don't you have a blessing left for me? . . . Do you have only one blessing Father? Bless me too, Father! And Esau raised his voice and wept . . . .

Esau harbored a grudge against Jacob because of the blessing that his father had given him, and Esau said to himself, When my father dies, I will kill my brother Jacob. Rebecca heard about what her elder son Esau was saying, so she sent for her younger son Jacob and said to him, Your brother Esau is planning to kill you. And now my son, listen to me and arise and flee to Laban my brother, to Haran. Stay with him for a few days until your brother's anger subsides—until your brother's anger with you subsides and he forgets what you did to him—and then I will send for you and bring you from there; why should I lose both of you in one day?

Rebecca said to Isaac, My life is miserable because of the Hittite girls; if Jacob takes a wife from Hittite girls like these, the girls of the land, what good is my life to me? So Isaac summoned Jacob and blessed him, and he charged him and said to him, Do not take a wife from among the Canaanite girls. Go to Padan Aram, to the house of Bethuel your mother's father, and take for yourself there a wife of the daughters of Laban, your mother's brother. And El Shaddai will bless you and will make you fruitful and will multiply you, and you will become a host of nations. He will give you the blessing of Abraham, to you and to your descendants, to inherit the land that you dwell in, that God gave to Abraham. Isaac sent Jacob away and he went to Padan Aram, to Laban the son of Bethuel the Aramean, the brother of Rebecca, Jacob's and Esau's mother.

Esau saw that Isaac blessed Jacob and sent him to Padan Aram to take a wife for himself there when he blessed him, and that he charged him and said, Do not take a wife from among the Canaanite girls . . . Esau saw that his father Isaac disliked the Canaanite girls; so Esau went to Ishmael and took as a wife Machalat the daughter of Ishmael the son of Abraham, the sister of Nevayot, in addition to his other wives. (26:34–28:9)

The story opens and closes with the wives that Esau chooses for himself. Esau's taking Hittite women, women of the land, has significance for the narrative of Jacob in two respects. First of all, like Esau's scorning of the birthright for a dish of food, his taking Canaanite girls is indicative of his unworthiness to assume the mantle of the Patriarch Abraham, for these actions of Esau betray a lack of concern for what happens to his descendants, a disregard for his future. In the previous generation, when Abraham had charged his servant with finding a wife for his son Isaac, the Patriarch had been absolutely unyielding in his insistence that Isaac not marry a Canaanite girl or return to the land of Abraham's origin, since either of these would have threatened the coming generations with assimilation among the surrounding idolaters:

> Abraham said to his servant . . . put your hand beneath my thigh and I will make you swear by the Lord, God of the heavens and God of the earth, that you will not take a wife for my son from the daughters of the Canaanites among whom I dwell . . . And the servant said to him, Perhaps the woman will not consent to go with me to this land, shall I return your son to the land from which you came? Abraham said to him, Beware lest you take my son back there . . . if the woman does not consent to go with you, you shall be free of this oath of mine; only do not take my son back there. (24:2–8)

Second, Esau's taking Hittite wives serves as Rebecca's pretext for having Isaac send Jacob away to her brother's house to find a wife, when her more pressing concern is really her fear that Esau will carry out the fratricidal intentions he justifiably harbors for his brother. This further manipulation of her husband by Rebecca is an indication of the obliquity of the relations between the parents of the twins, for Rebecca's role with respect to Isaac is that of the woman hidden from her man, like many of the other women in Genesis. Rebecca's pretext leads into Jacob's quest for his wives and fortune in Padan Aram, in the house of his uncle and father-in-law, Laban the Aramean. This quest encompasses his expiation for stealing Esau's blessing as well as his earning of his own blessing, and his transformation from hidden deceiver and follower to direct confronter, as we will see further on.

After the notice concerning Esau's marriages with Hittite women, the story continues with Isaac's announcement of his intention to bless Esau, the firstborn son. Rebecca, listening behind the scenes, takes matters into her own hands in her characteristically indirect way and tells Jacob to substitute himself for the absent Esau in order to receive the blessing in his stead. When she recounts Isaac's speech to Jacob, she quotes Isaac as saying "and I will bless you before the Lord," when he had actually said only "so that I may bless you." Perhaps this small change is meant to indicate that she has mistaken her husband's intention and believes that he wishes to give Esau the blessing of Abraham. That this is not Isaac's intention is clear from the words of the blessing itself, where there is no mention of Abraham's blessing of fertility and the gift of the land of Canaan. And in fact, it is only when Isaac blesses Jacob knowingly before sending him off to Padan Aram to find a wife that the blessing of Abraham is explicitly transmitted—to Jacob. A misunderstanding of Isaac's true wishes by Rebecca would be in keeping with the lack of direct communication between this husband and wife.

In any event, Rebecca tells Jacob to bring Isaac a meal that she will prepare in order to ensure that Jacob is the one to receive Isaac's blessing. This is the second time that Jacob uses food to procure for himself a privilege that belongs by right not to him, but to Esau—as he bought the birthright from Esau for the dish of lentil stew.

What is Jacob's role in the deception? Is he a willing accomplice, or is he manipulated by Rebecca, perhaps against his better judgment? The nature of Jacob's objection may reveal his view of her plan: "Jacob said to Rebecca his mother, But my brother Esau is a hairy man, while I am a smooth man. Perhaps my father will feel me and he will think me a trickster, and I will bring on myself a curse and not a blessing." One way of reading this is that Jacob is apparently concerned only with the practical problem of being discovered by his father, and being cursed as a result—not with the wrongness of what she wants him to do. For a practical problem Rebecca has a practical solution: She will cover Jacob's smooth skin with goat hair and will in addition give him Esau's clothes to wear in order to deceive Isaac. Incidentally, Jacob's description of himself as "a smooth man" carries some ironic overtones, for the Hebrew term for "smooth," like the English word, can have connotations of deceptive glibness (for example, "Falsely they speak to one another, smooth speech . . . ." in Psalms 12:3).

Alternatively, perhaps Jacob is reluctant to perpetrate what his mother has in mind, and his objection is a respectful way to evade her exhortations, since he cannot very well upbraid his mother for her objectionable proposal. Unfortunately, his mother comes up with a strategy that he cannot easily refute. On this reading, his failing is one of weakness rather than eager collaboration. In either case, his desire for his brother's portion has already been attested by his grasping of Esau's heel at their birth and by his extortionate purchase of the birthright, so Rebecca's idea cannot have been completely unwelcome.

In contrast to Jacob's smoothness, Esau is called a "hairy man." Esau's hairiness was noted at his birth: "The first emerged ruddy, his whole body like a cloak of hair . . ." (25:25). The Hebrew word for "hairy" with which Jacob describes his brother, Sa'iR, is mirrored in the name of the region (Se'iR) where Esau and his descendants dwell (32:4; 36:8–9), and, in addition means both "goat" and one of the satyr-like demons that cavort in the fields (Leviticus 17:7; Isaiah 13:21), as Esau is himself "a man of the field" (25:27). The association of the goat with Esau and Jacob's disguise of goatskins underlie later appearances of goats in subsequent deceptions in Genesis, as we will see.

When Jacob presents himself to his blind old father, Isaac senses that something is amiss, for the smooth voice and the hairy arms do not match. Isaac, having tested Jacob with two of his remaining senses—touch and smell—proceeds to bless him, thanks to Rebecca's clever disguise.

Esau's return is marked by a replay of the beginning of the preceding conversation with Jacob, but only up to a point. With Jacob we read, "He came to his father and he said, Father, and he said, Yes; who are you, my son?" The affection and benignity of this question are missing in Isaac's response to Esau: "His father Isaac said to him, Who are you?" Isaac's initial pathetic bewilderment gives way to shock when he hears Esau's reply, "I am your firstborn son Esau. Isaac was seized with a great trembling . . . ."

The moving scene of Esau's hurt and disappointment incorporates verbal signposts that point to later events in the developing saga of injustice, expiation, and transformation. Esau plays on

Jacob's name—"He is indeed called Jacob (Ya'aQoB); he has tricked me (VaYa'aQBeNi) now twice." Jacob received his name, we recall, because he emerged from the womb grasping the heel ('eQeB) of Esau. The heel is the site of the serpent's bite, the part of the body that is most easily accessible to an attacker lurking unseen in the grass, the place where he strikes after the victim has already passed by and is directing his attention elsewhere. Hence the serpent's curse in the Garden of Eden: "He will strike your head and you will strike his heel" (Genesis 3:15), and, in the patriarchal blessings that Jacob bestows on his sons at the end of his life: "May Dan be a serpent . . . who bites the heels of the horse, and his rider falls backward" (49:17).

Further play on Jacob's name will occur later on, when the text comes back to the second of the verbal signposts in Esau's speech—the words for birthright and blessing—for, as Esau says, ". . . he took my birthright (BêKoRaTi) and now he has taken my blessing (BiRKaTi)."

There is one more significant expression that will return later on when the tables are turned on Jacob: Isaac says, "Your brother came deceitfully . . ." using the word BêMiRMa, "with deceit." We will see the root RMH appear again later, when Laban cheats Jacob in a singularly appropriate manner.

The always-alert Rebecca, informed of Esau's intention to kill Jacob, sets about once again to help Jacob by manipulating Isaac, and arranges to have Jacob sent to her brother's home in Haran—ostensibly to find a wife. It is at this point that Isaac passes on to Jacob the blessing of Abraham. Jacob then undertakes his journey to Haran, there to undergo his expiation at the hands of his uncle Laban.

Once in Haran, Jacob enters into a relation of servant to master with his "brother" Laban—". . . You are my brother; should you work for me for nothing?" (29:15)—in order to earn the hand of Laban's younger daughter, Rachel. Jacob's servitude to Laban begins his expiation for stealing the blessing in which Isaac had unwittingly made Esau subservient to Jacob ("Be a master to your brothers, and your mother's sons will bow down to you" [27:29]). Jacob agrees to work for Laban for seven years as the price he is willing to pay for Rachel. How does Laban reward the seven years of servitude?

> Laban assembled all the people of the place and made a feast. When it was evening, he took his daughter Leah and brought her to him [i.e., to Jacob], and he cohabited with her . . . Then in the morning—it was Leah! He said to Laban, What is this that you have done to me? It was for Rachel that I worked for you; why did you deceive me?
>
> Laban said, It is not done so in our place, to give [or "to put"] the younger before the elder. (29:22–26)

By substituting the older sister for the younger in Jacob's nuptial tent, Laban has simply reversed the deception that his sister Rebecca had instigated with her sons. Laban's answer to Jacob is striking: "It is not done so in our place . . . ." In Canaan, perhaps, the younger may push himself ahead of the older, but not here. This is what Jacob must have heard, whatever Laban's intention may have been. The irony is even greater, for in being deceived by Laban as he had earlier deceived his father, Jacob has actually acquired the portion of the firstborn without wanting it—he has worked seven years for the younger sister, Rachel, but is then awarded her older sister. Jacob's complaint "Why did you deceive me?" is in Hebrew LaMa RiMiTaNi; the root signifying deceit is once again RMH, as it was used by Isaac in describing Jacob's deception. Laban then extracts seven additional years of servitude from Jacob in return for the woman he had wanted in the first place.

After both sisters are married to Jacob, it is on Leah the elder, "the unloved one," that God bestows the blessing of children, while the younger Rachel remains barren. In the marathon of childbearing that ensues in Genesis 29 and 30, Leah roundly trounces Rachel by coming in with six sons and a daughter to Rachel's one belated son, without counting the contributions of the maidservant-concubines.

In the next part of Jacob's struggle with his uncle, he must serve him for an additional six years in order to earn a blessing of wealth of his own (30:27–43). Hence, by the end of his stay with Laban, Jacob has acquired, besides wives and children, sizeable flocks and herds with which he will later attempt to repay Esau for the stolen blessing. We will deal with Jacob's meeting with Esau in detail later on.

Red and White, Goatskins and Goats

Based only on a straightforward reading of the text, we see an obvious relationship between Jacob's actions toward his brother and what he suffers at the hands of Laban. In addition, however, the text makes use of a symbolic opposition—between the colors red and white— to point to the same conclusions, as if to make it absolutely certain that there be no mistake in our reading of the story. We saw earlier that Esau was associated with redness, both at his birth ("The first emerged ruddy . . ."), and then later on, when Jacob buys the birthright from him—"Esau said to Jacob, Give me some of this red, red stuff (HaADoM HaADoM) to swallow because I'm famished, and this is why he is called Edom ('red')." In both of these instances what is at issue is the birthright, for at the time of their emergence from the womb, Jacob was found grasping the heel of Esau in an attempt to precede him. Color imagery is picked up in the story of Jacob's sojourn in Haran, for the name of his uncle, Laban (LaBaN), means "white."

The root meaning "white" in a verbal construction has the sense of "to purify," i.e., to make white or clean. Red, on the other hand, is the color that symbolizes sin in later prophetic and rabbinic literature, presumably because of its association with blood. The transformation of red to white is a metaphor for atonement for wrongdoing, as in the well-known verse from Isaiah, "If your sins be as scarlet they will become white as snow; if they be red as crimson they will become as wool" (1:18). Thus, Jacob's sin against Esau/Edom, the red brother, is expiated in the treatment he receives from his uncle Laban "the white."

The rabbinic literature of a much later age incorporated the imagery of the change from red to white as an expression for atonement for sin in the ritual of the scapegoat that is performed on the Day of Atonement. Here we return also to the association of Esau with the goat that we discussed earlier. As described in the Mishna and Talmud, the goat (Sa'iR, "hairy one") that is sent out to the wilderness has a shock of red wool tied between its horns before it is pushed to its death. When forgiveness for the sins of the Children of Israel has been attained, the red wool turns white (Babylonian Talmud [BT]

Yoma 67a). Thus, it appears that Jacob's actions and his expiation are archetypes of sin and atonement, and that both the redness of Esau and his hairiness are called upon in the ritual of the scapegoat.[1] Similarly, the use of a goat as the standard sin-offering in the Book of Leviticus and elsewhere may also have reference to Jacob's sin against his brother.

Redness and goats reappear in the sequelae of the struggle between Jacob and Esau, in the context of the story of Jacob's son Joseph. When Joseph, the younger son favored by his father Jacob, is sold into slavery by his resentful brothers, they deceive their father by slaughtering a goat and dipping Joseph's unique coat in the blood so that Jacob will think that he has been killed by a wild animal. The coat, Jacob's special gift marking the special affection he holds for Joseph, is the signal accompanying the brothers' demand to their father:

> Recognize [HaKeR Na], is this the coat of your son or not? He recognized it and said, It is my son's coat. A wild beast has eaten him; Joseph has fallen prey. (37:32–33)

The demand to recognize is an implicit demand that Jacob recognize his own responsibility for Joseph's putative death, for Jacob is once again guilty of putting the younger before the elder, thus fostering the animosity among the brothers. And the deception carried out by the sons' presentation to their father of Joseph's garment dipped in goat's blood—hairy goat (Sa'iR), red blood—conjures up the deception that Jacob perpetrated on his father by serving him a dish of goat meat disguised as game and by disguising himself with Esau's garments and with goatskins.

Since Jacob does not know that the blood he sees comes from a goat and not from his son, the irony here appears to be directed solely to the reader. However, there is something in the demand "to recognize" that might have reminded Jacob of his own deception of his father. The odd expression "is this the coat of your son or not?" seems incongruously callous in its peremptoriness, until we remember that when Isaac was trying to convince himself that the disguised Jacob was in reality Esau, he said to Jacob: "Come near and let me feel you, my son—are you my son Esau or not?" The concluding "or not" in a direct question is a rare construction, and might perhaps serve to stir Jacob's memory of his own misdeed.

A goat appears once more in the episode of Judah and Tamar that takes place after the sale of Joseph (Genesis 38). Tamar's disguise, by means of which she tricks Judah into making her pregnant, involves her setting aside her widow's garments and covering herself with a veil—a further instance of the use of a garment for purposes of deception. Judah agrees to give her a goat-kid as her harlot's fee, but when he attempts to have it delivered she is not there to accept it.

When she later presents him with the physical evidence proving that he is the one who made her pregnant, she too calls upon him to "Recognize," using the same words that the brothers had spoken to their father Jacob—HaKeR Na. Here as well, the call to recognize demands an acknowledgment of responsibility, in this case both for his impregnation of Tamar and, implicitly, for his role in Jacob's bereavement (as we will see in our chapter on Joseph).

The products of the union of Judah and Tamar are twin boys whose struggle at birth echoes the similar struggle that took place at the birth of Jacob and Esau:

> While she was giving birth he put out his hand, and the midwife took a red thread [ŠaNi] and tied it on his hand to signify "This one came out first [RIŠoNa]." But as he pulled his hand back, his brother emerged . . . . (38:28–29)

The red thread is intended to be a marker for the twin who looks to be the firstborn, but whose place is usurped by his energetic sibling. Thus the red thread—ŠaNi—comes to signify not RIŠoN, "first," as originally intended, but, in a striking word play, ŠeNi, meaning "second." The name of the boy with the red thread on his hand is ZeRaḤ, from a root denoting the shining of the rising sun—whose early meaning was "red." In this case, the red brother never owns the birthright at all. And in contrast to Jacob, who came out grasping his brother's heel, the child who supplants ZeRaḤ is called PeReṢ— the one who "burst forth" to emerge ahead of his twin. PeReṢ is the ancestor of the royal line of King David (Ruth 4:18–22).

Starting Over

There is a structure to the story of Jacob's adventures that expresses the circularity in the process of expiation that Jacob must undergo, as though he must travel a long distance simply in order to get back to his starting point. When Jacob stops for the night in his journey from Canaan to Padan Aram, he takes a stone and places it at his head and then dreams the dream of a ladder with angels ascending and descending. In the dream, God appears to him and promises that He will accompany him wherever he goes and will return him safely to his homeland. When Jacob awakes, he sets up the stone as a pillar, anoints it, and names the place Bethel, "House of God" (Genesis 28).

At the next stage of his journey Jacob continues on to the land of the Easterners, where he meets his future wife:

> He saw a well in the field and there were three flocks of sheep lying there beside it because from that well they would water the flocks, and the stone on the mouth of the well was large. All the flocks would gather there and they would roll [VêGaLêLu] the stone off the mouth of the well and water the sheep, and then would put the stone back in its place on the mouth of the well. Jacob said to them, My brothers, where are you from? . . . He said, It is still early, it is not yet time to take the cattle home, water the sheep and go and pasture. They said, We cannot, until all the flocks gather and they roll [VêGaLêLu] the stone off the mouth of the well and then we water the sheep.
>
> He was still speaking with them when Rachel came with her father's sheep, since she was a shepherdess. When Jacob saw Rachel the daughter of Laban his mother's brother, and the sheep of Laban his mother's brother, Jacob stepped up and rolled [VaYaGeL] the stone off the mouth of the well and watered [VaYaŠQ] the sheep of Laban his mother's brother. And Jacob kissed [VaYiŠaQ] Rachel and he raised his voice and wept. (29:2–11)

The daughter and the flocks of his uncle Laban inspire Jacob to perform what is apparently a great feat of strength in rolling the stone off the well in order to help Rachel by watering his uncle's sheep. The parallel treatment of Laban's daughter and his sheep is also conveyed in the similar words for Jacob's actions with respect to the two, in the orthographically identical VaYaŠQ, "he watered," and VaYiŠaQ, "he kissed." It is also probably not accidental that the name Rachel (RaHeL) means "ewe" (see 31:38, "Your ewes [RêHeLeKa] and your she-goats did not miscarry").

In the continuation of the story, Jacob works seven years for each of Laban's daughters and six years for a portion of his own from among the flocks of Laban, and then leaves his uncle's house with his wives, children, and flocks. Jacob's departure from Padan Aram is accomplished without Laban's knowledge, however:

> Jacob stole away from Laban the Aramean and did not tell him that he was running away. He ran away, he and all that were with him, and he arose and crossed the river, and he started out toward Mount Gilead. (31:20–21)

When Laban discovers his son-in-law's flight, he pursues him and catches up with him at Mount Gilead. After some mutual recrimination, they make a pact at Laban's suggestion:

> Now let us make a pact, you and I, and it will be a witness between us. Jacob took a stone and set it up as a pillar. Jacob said to his kinsmen [lit. "brothers"], Collect stones, and they took stones and made a cairn [GaL], and they ate there at the cairn. Laban called it YêGaR SaHaDuTa ["cairn of witness" in Aramaic], and Jacob called it GaL'eD ["cairn of witness" in Hebrew; play on Gilead].
>
> Laban said, This cairn [GaL] is a witness between us today, which is why its name is GaL'eD. Of the high place [MiŞPa, a high place suitable for scouting the surrounding country] he said, The Lord will look out [YiŞeP, "will watch"] between us if we conceal ourselves from one another....
>
> Laban said to Jacob, Here is this cairn [GaL] and here is this pillar [MaŞeBa, perhaps connected to MiŞPa] that I have set up between us. This cairn [GaL] is a witness and this pillar [MaŞeBa] is a witness that I will not cross this cairn [GaL] to you, and that you will not cross this cairn [GaL] and this pillar [MaŞeBa] to me to do ill....
>
> Jacob went on his way and angels of God met him. Jacob said when he saw them, This is the camp [or "host", MaHaNe] of God, and he called the name of the place MaHaNaYiM ["two camps"]. (31:44–32:3)

Jacob's crossing of the river here marks his leaving behind his father-in-law and the retribution that he has suffered at his hands. The meeting and struggle with Laban, and Laban's final acquiescence to Jacob's right to the fruits of his labors, are paralleled later on at the crossing of the YaBoQ river, where Jacob wrestles with an unnamed stranger before meeting his brother Esau for the first time in many years (we will discuss this episode shortly).

There are extensive parallels in the meeting with Laban to earlier episodes in Jacob's travails. Jacob sets up a pillar both after his dream at the outset of his journey to Haran and at his last leavetaking from Laban. The setting up of a pillar (MaSeBa) occurred in the first instance after his dream of angels ascending and descending the ladder (Genesis 28). The pillar at the meeting with Laban also follows a dream with an angel:

> An angel of God said to me in a dream, Jacob, and I said, Here I am. And he said, Raise your eyes and see, all the he-goats that are mounting the flocks are streaked, speckled, and spotted, for I have seen everything that Laban is doing to you. I am the God of Bethel, where you anointed a pillar, and where you made a vow to Me; now arise and leave this land and return to the land of your birth. (31:11–13)

This dream refers to the first pillar at Bethel, where God promised Jacob in a dream that He would be with him and would return him to his homeland; the later dream occurs at the time of the fulfillment of that promise, as does the erection of the second pillar at the meeting with Laban, when Jacob is in possession of a blessing that the Lord has granted him. Jacob's dream on his way to Haran is of angels going up and down a ladder, and on his final departure from Haran he is met by angels of God, whom he calls "the camp of God" (32:2–3). Entering and leaving Haran are both marked by dreams, angels, and pillars.

The symbolism of Jacob's actions at the meeting with Laban relates to Jacob's change in character. At the encounter with the shepherds on Jacob's arrival in Haran another stone had figured, the stone that covered the mouth of the well from which Jacob would water his future father-in-law's flocks. The Hebrew for Jacob's taking the stone off the mouth of the well is VaYaGeL—"he rolled" the stone—a verb from the same root that had already been used twice (VêGaLêLu) with reference to the stone blocking the well. The cairn that Jacob sets up on leaving Haran behind him is a GaL, the marker of separation between Jacob and Laban. The two similar expressions for rolling the stone and the pile of stones suggest reciprocal meanings that underlie Jacob's actions: Just as removing the stone from the well signifies his uncovering the source of the blessing that he would receive in Haran, so the erection of the pile of stones at the end of his sojourn with Laban signifies the replacement of the barrier between Jacob and the birthplace of Laban and Rebecca. For just as Haran is the source of blessing for Jacob, so is it also the source of his flawed character, since it is on account of his Haranite mother—Laban's wily sister—that Jacob becomes trapped in the web of deceit that almost costs him his life. With his uncle, Jacob leaves behind in Haran his deceitfulness and his shame at having swindled his brother out of what was rightfully his.

The testimony that Laban and Jacob talk about on Mount Gilead is also testimony to the legitimacy of Jacob's claim to the blessing that he had acquired by his hard labor, a testimony that will be sealed when Jacob wrestles with another "man"—the supernatural being who grants him the blessing of a new name.

The theme of brotherhood and brotherliness that informs the story of Jacob—as it will later inform the story of Joseph—is also developed through the reenactment at Gilead of Jacob's first encounter with the shepherds at the well of Haran (Genesis 29). When Jacob meets the men congregating at the well, he addresses them as "my brothers," although he is himself actually an unknown outsider to them. The opposition between the united shepherds/brothers and the outsider Jacob is underlined by their answer to his question as to why they do not continue to pasture, but rather stand idly by at the well. They tell him that when all the flocks gather together, the company of shepherds rolls the enormous stone off the mouth of the well in concert, and then returns the stone to its place after all the flocks have drunk. However, as soon as Jacob sees his cousin Rachel approaching with his uncle's flocks, he goes up to the well and rolls the stone off single-handed. By this gesture, he accomplishes several things: He demonstrates that, even without brothers, he is as powerful as the band of shepherds; he himself becomes a "brother" by performing their joint task; and he thereby acquires for himself a special standing as brother to Rachel, supplanting her kinsmen as he will supplant her father and brothers in her loyalty later on.

At the final resolution of Jacob's conflict with Laban we have the meeting at Gilead and the setting up of the pillar and the cairn:

> Jacob took a stone and set it up as a pillar. Jacob said to his kinsmen [lit. "brothers"], Collect stones, and they took stones and made a cairn [GaL], and they ate there at the cairn. (31:45–46)

Now it is the brothers of Jacob who collectively participate in making the GaL, or pile of stones, and the outsider at this event is now Laban. And just as the stone at the well signified the opening of the way to the source of wealth in Haran, so now the stones at Gilead represent the closing of that way once more. At the meal at the cairn, Laban acquiesces to Jacob's taking away the wealth that he had earned in Haran. The transfer of blessings of material wealth has characteristically taken place at meals before now as well, both when Jacob extorted Esau's birthright from him in return for feeding him the lentils and bread, and then later when Isaac wished to bestow his blessing on Esau at the meal of game—when Jacob substituted himself for the hunter Esau and, analogously, the tame goat-kids for the wild game that Esau was to have served to his father.

There are a number of other ways in which the end of Jacob's stay in Haran mirrors its beginning. We saw Jacob water the flocks of Laban at his very entry into the land of his uncle, and we see him watering the flocks again at the end, when he ensures that he obtains his reward for his work with Laban (30:38). Corresponding to the celebration of Jacob's marriage to Laban's daughter and Laban's deceitful substitution of Leah for Rachel at the beginning of the episode, we later have Laban berating Jacob:

> Laban said to Jacob, What have you done? [as Jacob had said "What is this that you have done to me?" when Laban tricked him by substituting Leah for Rachel]. You have deceived me and have led my daughters away like captives of war. Why did you run away in secret, concealed from me, without telling me so that I could have sent you off with joy and songs, with drums and music? (31:26–27)

And, as we have seen, there are dreams, angels, and pillars both at the beginning and at the end.

The structure of these chapters reflects a journey out and the return over the same route on the way back. In the case of Jacob, this represents the long detour, or parenthesis, that requires him to travel a great distance in order to get back to where he started from. In order to achieve what he thought he could acquire through the short-cut of deceiving his father, he is now forced to take the long way—twenty years of servitude to his uncle, a combination of both brother and father figure—in order to earn a blessing that he can rightfully claim as his own. In the course of this story we witness Jacob's development from a man of devious means into one who can face directly first his uncle, then the supernatural being with whom he wrestles at the Jabbok River, and finally, his brother Esau.

Jacob's journey to Haran is a journey back to the source of blessing. Haran is where Abraham came from and where his family remains, and is the place to which Abraham sent his servant to find a wife for Isaac, as Jacob finds his wives there before returning to Canaan. Jacob's going back to Padan Aram is a retracing of the steps of Abraham, who had been told, "Go forth from your land and your birthplace and the house of your father to the land that I will show you" (12:1). Jacob's trip is a leaving of his birthplace, like Abraham's, but is also a return to the place of origin of his grandfather and his mother. In a way, then, Jacob's is a starting over from the beginning in a more radical sense than simply returning to the state that he himself started from; it is not only Jacob who starts anew, but the whole family of Abraham.

Why does the family have to start over? Because the transmission of the legacy of Abraham has been set back by Jacob's actions. When Jacob goes back to Haran he must be remade in the image of Abraham, who had to be separated from his place of origin while at the same time remaining apart from the culture of Canaan into which he was a newcomer. And, as we suggested in our preceding chapter, the reason that Jacob must return to his origins and start over begins with his father Isaac, who was himself shaped by the actions of *his* father, Abraham.

The Struggle for Blessing, Straightening the Crooked

The motif of expiation for wrongdoing that is developed in the story of Jacob's actions and tribulations is reinforced by means of color imagery—based on the names of Jacob's brother and uncle—that suggests the whitening of a red stain. Similarly, the development of the character of Jacob is accompanied by a series of word plays linking Jacob's name with ideas of following, deception, and struggle. The changing of Jacob's name that takes place at the dramatic climax of Jacob's transformation is expressed in terms of the opposition between crookedness and straightness, by means of plays on both his old name and his new name.

We mentioned earlier that the name Jacob, ostensibly related to the word 'eQeB, meaning "heel," has an additional association with another meaning of the same root—"crooked"—in addition to meaning "to follow," as one follows on the heels of a predecessor. When Esau commented bitterly on the deception perpetrated by his younger brother, he played on Jacob's name in its sense of trickery or deception: "He is indeed called Jacob (Ya'aQoB); he has tricked me (VaYa'aQBeNi) now twice" (27:36).

Plays on Jacob's name run through the story, marking the developments in Jacob's status and persona. Jacob's name comes from his grasping Esau's heel at birth, and his double tricking of Esau is expressed in the play Ya'aQoB/Ya'aQBeNi. Jacob is thus initially portrayed as a follower or pursuer who repeatedly attempts to push ahead of his elder brother, and then steals his blessing by trickery. His sojourn with his uncle Laban effects the transformation that will later be affirmed in the famous scene of Jacob's wrestling with the angel at the Jabbok River.

Jacob's twenty years of toil in Haran, besides comprising his expiation by being subjected to deception and servitude at the hands of Laban, also results in his acquisition by the sweat of his brow of his own blessing of wealth. The blessing he now owns is his by right; no one can accuse him of taking anything illicitly. Jacob's honest work thus also gives him a sense of legitimate ownership which he can defend against anyone who casts doubt on it—as he could not previously, when his blessing was acquired at his brother's expense by deceit.

Jacob's decision to take his wealth and leave Laban is hastened by the grumbling of Laban's sons and the sour countenance of his uncle:

> He heard the words of Laban's sons who were saying, Jacob has taken everything of our father's; it is from what belongs to our father that he has gained all this wealth. And Jacob saw that Laban's demeanor [lit. "face"] toward him was not as it had been before. (31:1–2)

Jacob consults with his wives and decides to leave Haran without Laban's knowledge, fleeing from Laban's hostile "face." When Laban learns of Jacob's flight, he rushes in pursuit and catches up with Jacob's party at Gilead, where, as we saw above, they set up a cairn and a pillar to seal a pact at their final parting. But before the two men come to this understanding, Laban rebukes Jacob for running away and carrying off his daughters without letting him know, and, in addition, accuses him of making off with his household gods (which Rachel has actually stolen, unbeknownst to Jacob). Jacob does not let Laban's tirade go unanswered:

> Jacob was angry and he quarreled with Laban; Jacob answered and said to Laban, What is my crime and what is my sin that you lit out after me? You've rummaged through all my goods—what have you found of all your household goods?—put it here right in front of my brothers and your brothers and let them judge between us. These twenty years that I've been with you, your ewes and she-goats didn't miscarry and I didn't eat any rams of your flocks. I didn't bring you any animal killed by beasts, I made up for it, you exacted it from me, whether it was taken by day or by night. Heat consumed me by day and frost by night, and sleep fled from my eyes. It's been twenty years that I've been in your house; I worked for you fourteen years for your two daughters and six years for your flocks, and you changed my wages ten times. If the God of my father, the God of Abraham and the Awe of Isaac, hadn't been with me you would have sent me away now empty-handed; God saw my suffering and my toil and gave judgment last night. (31:36–42)

Jacob's indignant speech lays out his claim to the wealth that he has acquired and demonstrates his readiness to confront Laban face to face to defend it, in contrast to his initial impulse to flee from Laban's angry "face." The long struggle with Laban is the beginning of Jacob's conditioning for his eventual meeting with Esau, where, as we will soon see, the motif of face-to-face confrontation is developed more explicitly.

The second stage in Jacob's preparation for facing Esau involves another struggle, this time face to face with a divine being.

In Genesis 32, after having left Laban and immediately before meeting Esau for the first time in twenty years, Jacob transports his family and flocks over the river at the Jabbok crossing and remains alone that night. Ma'aBaR YaBoQ, the Jabbok crossing, is Jacob's Rubicon; the meeting with Esau is now unavoidable. YaBoQ is a play on Ya'aQoB, Jacob's name, and is the place where the change in Jacob's status is explicitly affirmed—the place where he completes his crossing over from the deceitful pursuer to the rightful holder of his own blessing. It is at this crossing that Jacob meets a nameless man/ God/angel who wrestles with him until the break of day and then gives him a new name with which he can face his brother:

> Jacob [Ya'aQoB] was left by himself, and a man wrestled [VaYeABeQ] with him until daybreak. He saw that he could not prevail over him, so he struck his hip-socket, and Jacob's [Ya'aQoB] hip-socket[2] was pulled out of joint in his wrestling [BêHeABQo] with him. He said, Let me go, for daylight has come; and he said, I will not let you go unless you bless me. He said to him, What is your name? And he said, Jacob [Ya'aQoB]. He said, It will no longer be said, Your name is Jacob [Ya'aQoB, "crooked"], but Israel [YiSRaEL], for you have contended [SaRITa] with a divine being [or "God," ELoHiM] and with men and you have prevailed. (32:25–29)

Jacob's wrestling with the supernatural being plays on his name: VaYeABeQ, "he wrestled," echoes the VaYa'aQBeNi of Jacob's tricking of Esau, and both play on the name Jacob. When the stranger changes Jacob's name he does not use the usual verb QRA, "to call," in saying that his name will no longer be called Jacob, but rather the verb AMR, "to say," which requires that the phrase be translated as "It will no longer be said, Your name is Ya'aQoB." In other words, it is not simply Jacob's name that is changed, but also his reputation as a trickster. People will no longer say "Your name is Jacob, the crooked one," as Esau had done earlier. There is an additional association with one of the other meanings of the root, "to follow," for Jacob will henceforth no longer be regarded as a mere follower, in envious pursuit of his elder brother. Jacob's struggles with men refer to his past struggle with Laban, in which Jacob prevailed, and to his struggle with Esau, in which he is reassured that he will likewise prevail—as he prevailed in his struggle with the mysterious adversary.[3]

Jacob's new name is Israel, YiSRaEL, "For you have contended (SaRiTa)." However, YiSRaEL, "Israel," is orthographically identical to a word that could be read YaŠaREL, from the root YŠR, meaning "straight." The transformation from crooked to straight in the story of Jacob invokes the same dichotomy between 'QB and YŠR that appears in Isaiah (40:4): "The rugged ground (lit. "the crooked," He'aQoB) shall become level (lit. "straight," LêMiŠoR)." A third name that Jacob is called in a more poetic context is YêŠuRuN, also from the root meaning "straight," in Deuteronomy (32:15 and 33:5) and in Isaiah (44). The poetic parallelism between Israel and Yeshurun in Isaiah suggests that the association of Israel with the root for "straight" had not escaped some of the biblical authors:

> Now listen Jacob my servant, and Israel whom I have chosen. Do not be afraid my servant Jacob, and Yeshurun whom I have chosen. (Isaiah 44:1–2)

The crossing at Jabbok is the site of Jacob's transformation from 'aQoB, "crooked," to YaŠaR, "straight."[4] This is the final step in the process of Jacob's leaving behind his name of "crooked"—the process that had begun twenty years earlier when he arrived at his uncle's house in Haran.

Wrestling and Embracing

It is now twenty years since Jacob stole Esau's blessing and fled from his wrath. On his way back to his homeland, Jacob has overpowered a divine adversary in a face-to-face encounter and is now prepared to finally meet Esau:

> Jacob looked up and saw Esau approaching with four hundred men, so he divided the children up with Leah and with Rachel and with the two

maidservants . . . He passed in front of them and bowed to the ground seven times until he approached his brother. Esau ran to meet him, and embraced him [VaYêHaBQeHu], and he fell on his neck and kissed him, and they wept. (33:1–4)

The word for "embracing," VaYêHaBeQ, is related both phonetically and etymologically to the word for "wrestling," VaYeABeQ, as indeed an embrace can signify either combat or love. The evolution in the meanings of Jacob's name is thus from following ('eQeB, "heel"), to deception (VaYa'aQBeNi), to striving (VaYeABeQ), to the forgiveness of Esau's embrace (VaYêHaBQeHu). Thus, as in the story of Noah and the Flood, the last word play in the series signals forgiveness and reconciliation. We will see a similar progression expressed through plays on another root when we discuss the story of Joseph.

But the embrace refers in a subtle way to the wrestling of the younger with the older that is the backdrop for the story of Jacob. The connection between the two encounters becomes clearer if we visualize the two scenes as occurring one after the other. First Jacob is locked in combat with the divine being, and next he is locked in an embrace with his brother Esau. We will see shortly that there are other ways in which the meeting with Esau refers back to the wrestling with the angel, indicated in the naming of the place where the wrestling takes place—"Peniel/Penuel," meaning "the face of God."

To return to the embrace of the brothers: There are only two other occurrences of similar forms of the verb "to embrace" in the entire Pentateuch (actually in the whole Hebrew Bible), both of them in connection with Jacob, and both playing on the name Ya'aQoB. One precedes Jacob's meeting with Esau and the other follows much later, but both appear in the context of the competition between older and younger siblings and the substitution of the younger for the elder that is the hallmark of the story of Jacob. At Jacob's first meeting with his uncle Laban we read:

When Laban heard the news of Jacob his sister's son he ran to meet him, and he embraced [VaYêHaBeQ] him and kissed him, and brought him into his house . . . . (29:13)

This embrace is a preface to the tribulations that Laban will inflict on Jacob, in the course of which Jacob's servitude to his "brother"

132

Laban is accompanied by the substitution of the elder sister for the younger and results in Jacob's acquisition of a blessing that he later offers to Esau in symbolic restitution.

The other embrace appears in Genesis 48, in the account of Jacob's blessing of the sons of Joseph in Egypt:

> Israel saw the sons of Joseph and said, Who are these? Joseph said to his father, They are my sons . . . he said, Bring them to me and I will bless them. Israel's eyes were dim with age—he could not see—and he brought them near to him, and he kissed them and embraced them [VaYêHaBeQ] . . . Israel put forth his right hand and put it on Ephraim's head even though he was the younger, and his left on Menashe's head; he crossed his hands, for Menashe was the firstborn . . . Joseph said to his father, Not so, Father, this one is the firstborn, put your right hand on his head. But his father demurred and said, I know my son, I know; he too will become a nation and he too will be great, but his younger brother will be greater than he and his descendants will be numerous among the nations. (48:8–19)

Here the significance of the embrace is more explicit, as though to say that the patriarch "Jacobed" the boys, which he does by subtly crossing his arms over their heads in order to make sure that the younger son takes precedence over the firstborn.

There are many other meetings in the Pentateuch that could have been accompanied by embraces, but it is only with Jacob that we find the word VaYêHaBeQ (or VaYêHaBQeHu), pointing to the special nature of these particular embraces and to their connection with elements that are uniquely associated with Jacob's struggles. Jacob's embraces are fraught with ambivalence; they ring with overtones of the competition—the wrestling—that goes on constantly between the younger brother and the older.

Face and Heel

The significance of Jacob's wrestling with the stranger is expressed in yet another way that clarifies its relationship to the meeting with Esau. Before the encounter at Jabbok, Jacob prepares to meet his brother for the first time after having stolen his blessing twenty years earlier. Jacob first sends messengers to see if he can divine Esau's intentions. The messengers return saying that Esau is approaching with an army of four hundred men, news that brings fear to Jacob's heart. He takes precautions in order to safeguard his family, prays to God, and prepares a gift that he sends ahead to propitiate his brother:

> He slept there that night, and took of what he had with him as a gift for his brother Esau: Two hundred she-goats and twenty he-goats [a list of the various gifts follows] . . . And you shall say, Here your servant Jacob too is behind us; for he thought, I will appease him [AKaPRa PaNaV] with the gift that goes before me [LêPaNai] and then I will face him [lit. "see his face," PaNaV], perhaps he will favor me [YiSA PaNai]. And the gift passed before him ['aL PaNaV], and he was going to sleep in the camp that night. (32:14–22)

Jacob's thoughts express his fear in an interesting way. The Hebrew words that I have transliterated in the brackets all contain forms of the word for "face," PaNiM, alternating repeatedly between "his face" and "my face." The remarkable repetition of these words here conveys exactly what it is that is on Jacob's mind: He is worried about facing Esau directly, without any advantage or disguise, not deviously or deceitfully, not by grasping his heel from behind. The wrestling with the stranger is a playing out of Jacob's confronting this fear. When it is clear that Jacob has "the man" in his power, he demands, and receives, a blessing from him—not by pretending to be Esau as he had once done, but by virtue of his own struggling and prevailing. The man's blessing is expressed as the changing of Jacob's name from "crooked" to "straight," enabling him to meet Esau on new terms now.

After the struggle with the stranger, Jacob gives the place of the encounter a name:

> Jacob called the name of the place Peniel ["face of God"], for I saw God [or "a divine being"] face to face [PaNiM EL PaNiM] and I survived. (32:31)

With the confidence gained in this supernatural face-to-face encounter, Jacob can now face his brother on the plane of a more mundane reality.

The two brothers meet and embrace, an act that resonates with some irony as we saw, and Jacob presses his gift—or, as he calls it, his "blessing"—on his brother:

Jacob said, Please do not [refuse]; if I have found favor in your eyes please accept my gift from me, for I regard you as I would God [RaITi PaNeKa KiRêOT PêNe ELoHiM—lit. "I see your face as seeing the face of God"], and you have favored me. Please take my blessing [BiRKaTi] that has been brought to you, for God has been gracious to me and I have everything; and he insisted, and he accepted. (33:10–11)

Jacob can face Esau as he has already faced both his uncle Laban and an angel/God, without fear. The two expressions "for I saw God face to face and I survived" and "for I see your face as seeing the face of God, and you have favored me" spell out the change in Jacob's relationship to Esau, and indeed in his relationship to any adversary. At the same time, his insistence that Esau accept his "blessing" from him represents restitution of the blessing that he had stolen from Esau twenty years ago. What had hitherto been called a "gift" is unusually called a "blessing" by Jacob when he presses it on Esau, signifying its relation to the stolen blessing that had been the cause of the long separation between the brothers. Jacob has by now earned his own blessing through the twenty years of servitude in his uncle's house, a blessing that has been acknowledged not only by his uncle but also by no less than a supernatural being—the angel/God with whom Jacob has done battle. Esau's acceptance of the gift signals the end of the conflict over the stolen blessing.

And yet, despite Esau's gracious overlooking of past wrongs, Jacob still maintains his distance from his brother, for when Esau offers to travel with him—or at least to lend him the support of some of his warriors—Jacob makes excuses and goes off on his own while Esau returns to his home in Seir (33:12–17). The relationship between the brothers has come a long way from its outright fratricidal stage, although, as is generally true of fraternity in the Book of Genesis, it never achieves real warmth.

Close Encounters

The dramatic turning point of the Jacob narrative is his dreamlike wrestling, alone and at night, with the stranger at Jabbok, while the immediately following meeting with Esau—in which the real resolution of the fraternal conflict occurs—is practically anticlimactic by comparison. There are two other occurrences in the Pentateuch of such supernatural encounters that precede fateful meetings in ordinary human reality, and all three exemplify a pattern of conflict and resolution that sets the stage for the meetings that follow.

To recapitulate briefly, Jacob, on his way home from Haran, wrestles with a man/God/angel who wounds him in the thigh, an injury that may foreshadow the strife among his sons in the next generation. Reassured by his successful struggle with the angel, Jacob is ready to face his brother Esau as he had never before been able to face him, and then to make symbolic restitution of the blessing that he had stolen from him.

The next supernatural encounter is found near the beginning of the Book of Exodus and involves Moses and his wife and son, who are on their way to Egypt from Midian. Let us review in outline the story of Moses before his return to Egypt to confront the obdurate Pharaoh and to liberate the Israelites from their bondage (Exodus 2–4).

While still a member of Pharaoh's household, Moses goes out to "his brothers"—slaves of the Egyptians—and intervenes twice to rescue an oppressed slave from his antagonist, who is an Egyptian in the first case and a fellow slave in the second. As a result of a Hebrew slave's reporting the killing of the Egyptian by Moses to Pharaoh, Moses is forced to flee the land of his birth. He comes to Midian, where he finds himself at the well where the shepherds gather to water their flocks. He sees the male shepherds of Midian drive away the defenseless shepherdesses, the daughters of Jethro, when the latter attempt to water their father's flocks. He rescues them from the male shepherds and waters the flocks for them. As a result of his brave action, he is invited to dwell with Jethro and is rewarded with the hand of Jethro's daughter Zipporah in marriage. Moses stays on, tending the flocks of his father-in-law, and two sons are eventually born to him and his wife.

One day, while tending the flocks, he sees a vision of a burning bush and hears the voice of God telling him to return to Egypt and to free His people from their bondage. After being armed with a number of signs with which to impress both the Hebrews and the Egyptians, he reluctantly agrees to return to Egypt on his mission of liberation.

He prepares to go, tells his father-in-law that he must go to see how his "brothers" in Egypt are faring, and takes his wife and sons with him on the return to Egypt. And then, on the way, when they stop for the night, God attempts to kill him:

> It was on the road, at the night encampment [MaLoN], the Lord met him and sought to kill him. Zipporah took a flint and cut off the foreskin of her son, and touched his legs, and said, For a bridegroom of blood are you to me; when He let him alone she said, A bridegroom of blood of circumcision [MuLoT]. (4:24–26)

Moses, unlike Jacob, cannot overcome his adversary, but must be rescued by means of a symbolic sacrifice of his eldest son, performed by Zipporah, who thereby makes Moses her "bridegroom of blood." After this, Moses continues on his way, and is met by his elder brother, Aaron, together with whom he goes on—first to approach the Israelites and then to confront Pharaoh.

I suggest that the "bridegroom of blood" interlude is the story of the symbolic price that Moses must pay for his reluctance to carry out the mission for which God had called to him from the flame. Some support for this interpretation is found in the context in which this mysterious episode appears. Right before the "bridegroom of blood" encounter God tells Moses to deliver the following message to Pharaoh:

> Tell Pharaoh, Thus said the Lord, Israel is My firstborn son. I have said to you, Release My son that he may serve Me, and you have refused to release him; so I will kill your firstborn son. And it was on the road, at the night encampment . . . . (4:22–24)

Since Moses had not wished to rescue the firstborn son of God— Israel—from Egypt, God exacts from him his own firstborn son, albeit symbolically, as the destroying God will later take all the firstborn sons of the Egyptians. The shedding of the blood of Moses' firstborn is a prefiguring of the apotropaic lamb's blood on the Israelite doorjambs, the blood that will protect the firstborn sons of the Hebrews from the fate that overtakes the Egyptian firstborn.[5]

When summarized in this fashion, the parallels between the stories of Jacob and Moses are quite obvious. Both flee to a foreign land to escape a threat to their lives that originates—either directly or indirectly—with their brothers; both perform notable feats in watering the flocks of shepherdesses who later become their wives; both tend the sheep of their fathers-in-law in the foreign country, have children, and then—in response to a divine command—set out to return to their native countries. In both cases, they are uncertain of the reception they will receive at the hands of those who had once threatened their lives. And, in both cases, a mysterious struggle with a divine being/God occurs before they face their adversaries, resulting in a wounding that is symbolically related to their offspring.

In each of the stories, the particular significance of the struggle is related to the particular circumstances in which the protagonist is placed, or in which he has placed himself. Jacob must be fully prepared to face—and to make at least token reparation to—the brother whom he had swindled twenty years earlier, and Moses must himself be cleared of the sin for which Pharaoh and the Egyptians will later be punished.

But the aspects of the struggles that are shared bespeak a more general, paradigmatic role of the struggle. The preternatural encounter with the divine force is in both instances a prelude to a fateful encounter with a human adversary. The protagonist has reason to dread the encounter in the real world, and the preliminary meeting and struggle is a preparation for the second meeting; only after the first confrontation is successfully concluded can the second one take place. This preparation can be seen from one point of view as psychological—cleansing and empowering the hero before the real encounter in order to ensure that he is able to mobilize his full strength.

In the case of Jacob, what must be overcome is his fear of Esau, which is rooted in his underlying realization that Esau is really right and he is really wrong. Therefore, the man/God with whom he wrestles and over whom he prevails blesses him by giving him a new name that affirms his transformation from the pursuer of Esau to the owner of a blessing of his own that he can defend with a clear conscience. His ability to confront "Elohim" face to face is his assurance that he will also be able to meet his brother face to face.

In Exodus, the unsatisfactory response of Moses to God's call reflects Moses' lack of confidence in himself—"Who am I to go to Pharaoh?" (Exodus 3:11); "But they won't believe me and they won't listen to me . . ." (4:1); and "Please, Lord, I am not a man of words . . . I am slow of speech and slow of tongue" (4:10)—which prevents him from showing the necessary degree of concern for his enslaved brothers. His reluctance to rescue the firstborn of God is atoned for by his giving up his own firstborn to God.

Both Jacob and Moses can now go on to meet their flesh-and-blood adversaries with a clear conscience. The basis for the psychological cleansing that is the result of the struggle with the divine antagonist is in both cases a moral cleansing. Jacob, having expiated his crime against his brother, is now the possessor of his own hard-earned blessing with which he can repay Esau; Moses, having paid for his own refusal to free the enslaved Hebrews, is now free to attack Pharaoh for the same sin.

In addition to the general idea of the pre-meeting as preparation for a real meeting, the means by which the preparation is achieved is of special interest. In both stories of the preparatory encounter a wound is inflicted: Jacob, wounded in the thigh, must limp afterward, while Moses is touched with the blood of the circumcision of his son by Zipporah. The wound in both cases represents on a somatic level the exorcism of the sin of which the protagonist must be cleansed before he can enter the field of the dreaded conflict. The flaw is concentrated, or focused, by being incarnated into a part of the body, and then extirpated—as though by surgery—with the infliction of the wound. The hero, having paid his price and been freed of his moral and psychological burden of guilt, can now meet his antagonist with a wholeness that he could not have mustered without this preparation.

A similar pattern of a preliminary encounter with a supernatural being preceding and preparing the stage for a meeting in the real world appears in the story of Balaam, the prophet of Pethor, in Numbers 22–24.

Balak, king of Moab, hearing of the unstoppable progress of the invading Israelites through the neighboring lands, fears for the safety of his own kingdom. He therefore sends messengers to recruit the prophet Balaam—renowned for his powers of both blessing and imprecation—to defeat the Israelites by invoking one of his powerful curses. Balaam is tempted by Balak's implied offer of remuneration, but must first wait for God's consent. God comes to him at night and tells him not to go, and Balaam is thus forced to reply to the royal messengers that, much as he personally would like to, he is unable to accommodate the king. Balak, assuming that Balaam's refusal is simply a bargaining ploy, sends higher-ranking emissaries and makes his offer more explicit. Balaam once again consults God, hoping that God has perhaps relented since the last time he heard from Him, and this time God permits him to go—but with the proviso that Balaam do only what God tells him. The well-known story continues as follows:

> Balaam arose in the morning, saddled his donkey, and went with the nobles of Moab. God was angry that he was going, and an angel of the Lord stood on the road to obstruct him as he was riding on his donkey accompanied by his two servants.
>
> The donkey saw the angel of the Lord standing on the road with his sword drawn in his hand, and the donkey swerved off the road and walked into the field; Balaam beat the donkey to make her turn back onto the road. The angel of the Lord stood in the vineyard path, with a wall on either side.
>
> The donkey saw the angel of the Lord and pressed herself against the wall, pressing Balaam's leg against the wall; and he beat her again. The angel of the Lord continued to pass [before them], and he stood in a narrow space where there was no room to turn, neither to the right nor to the left.
>
> The donkey saw the angel of the Lord and lay down under Balaam; and Balaam became angry and beat the donkey with the stick. The Lord opened the mouth of the donkey and she said to Balaam, What have I done to you, that you have beat me these three times? Said Balaam to the donkey, Because you have mocked me; if I had a sword in my hand, I would kill you now. And the donkey said to Balaam, Am I not your donkey, whom you have ridden always? Has it been my habit to do this to you? And he said, No.
>
> The Lord uncovered Balaam's eyes and he saw the angel of the Lord standing on the road with his sword drawn in his hand, and he bowed down and prostrated himself. The angel of the Lord said to him, Why did you beat your donkey these three times? It is I who have come out as an obstructer... The donkey saw me and swerved away from me these three times; if she hadn't swerved away from me, it would have been you that I would have killed now and I would have let her live.

Balaam said to the angel of the Lord, I am at fault, for I did not know that you were standing before me on the road; and now, if you disapprove, I will turn back. The angel of the Lord said to Balaam, Go with the men, but say only what I tell you to say; and Balaam went with Balak's nobles. (22:21–35)

In the subsequent verses we read of Balak's vain attempts to get Balaam to curse the Israelites, and how God puts other words—words of blessing—into Balaam's mouth, until Balaam finally accepts fully his role as God's messenger and blesses the Children of Israel in his own words.

The story of the mission of Balaam bears a formal resemblance to the account of God's appointment of Moses in Exodus 3 and 4—but the resemblance is most striking in the almost exact inversion of the story of Moses in the story of Balaam. Moses' mission is to save the Hebrews, while Balaam's appointment is to destroy them. In both cases there is a clash of wills between the prophet and God concerning the mission. In Exodus, God wants the prophet to go while the prophet himself is unwilling; in Numbers, it is the prophet who is eager while God is the reluctant one. Moses is elsewhere described as the most humble of men ("The man Moses was very humble, more than anyone else on earth" [Numbers 12:3]), while Balaam is hungry for wealth and honor (what other motive does he have for pestering God to allow him to accompany Balak's messengers?) and is given to self-vaunting ("The speech of Balaam, son of Beor / the speech of the man of unclouded eye / The speech of him who hears the words of God/ who sees the vision of Shaddai / who, though he falls, is open-eyed" [24:3–4, and similarly in 24:15–16]). Moses is clumsy of speech, inarticulate ("I am not a man of words . . . I am slow of speech and slow of tongue"), while Balaam declaims his piece in skillfully crafted couplets. Balaam piously and hypocritically repeats that he himself is really powerless, that he can do only what God tells him, while Moses is prepared to stand up even to God when God Himself threatens to destroy the Israelites.

In the story of Balaam and the donkey, the self-important seer is deflated. Even the donkey can see that God does not wish Balaam to curse the Hebrews, even the donkey can see the obstructing angel of God on the road—but Balaam, "the man of unclouded eye," cannot.

The donkey balks at the dire angel, but Balaam, in his blind eagerness to attain his reward, beats her to get her going again. He is mocked by the donkey, who—after dragging him in all directions and finally simply lying down under him in the road—bests him in an argument that is more comic than anything else. Balaam's struggle with his donkey falls solidly into the genre of slapstick.

But let us not lose sight of our reason for bringing up the story of Balaam and the donkey: the parallel with the story of Moses that includes a threatening supernatural encounter as a prelude to a fateful meeting. In the case of Moses, God meets him on the way and attempts to kill him, and he is rescued by his wife's performing a symbolic sacrifice of their firstborn son; in the story of Balaam, an angel of the Lord faces him with an unsheathed sword as he rides on *his* way, and Balaam is saved from death by his donkey, who injures Balaam's leg by pressing it against a wall. It may be that the donkey is killed in Balaam's place, although the text is ambiguous as to whether or not the angel kills the donkey (see the passage quoted above) and commentators are divided on this question.

The paradigm that unfolds in the three episodes of Jacob and the "man," Moses and God, and Balaam and the angel is clear in its main elements. The protagonist is on his way to a critical meeting, but his ability to carry out his mission is compromised by a conflict that first needs to be resolved. With Jacob the conflict is entirely internal—he fears Esau but he must approach nevertheless—while with Moses and Balaam the conflict is between the desires of the prophet and the wishes of God. The supernatural agent, or God himself, intervenes, and the conflict materializes into a physical struggle between the protagonist and an externalized adversary. In the course of the struggle, the conflict is resolved by an exorcism that involves the infliction of a wound—to Jacob's thigh, Moses' son, Balaam's leg (or his donkey)—thereby removing the potential obstacle. The injury/sacrifice/slaying removes the equivocal element that compromises the protagonist's effectiveness—by allaying Jacob's fears, by removing the source of guilt that would compromise Moses' moral authority, and by putting the fear of the Lord into Balaam, who, but for the grace of God, would have gone the way of his more perspicacious, but less fortunate, donkey. By the time the actual meeting takes place, its internally problematic aspects have already been defused in the prior supernatural confrontation.[6,7]

Cairns and Pillars

Having discussed at length Jacob's character and inner conflicts, let us now take up the thread of a different kind of symbolism that pervades his story. Each of the Patriarchs has associated with him a symbolic representation of his role. Abraham is a digger of wells and a builder of altars, signifying his role as source and origin of a new order as well as his more specific hieratic role as founder of a new cult. Isaac, as we have seen, redigs the wells of Abraham and gives them the same names that his father did, indications of his role of transmitter of the values of Abraham. As we will see in the next chapter, Joseph, the favored son and hated brother, is associated with clothing and changes of clothing, with cloaking and unmasking, which are expressions of, among other things, men's ignorance and awareness of God's participation in the affairs of mortals.

Jacob's significant object is the stone. He puts a stone under his head when he lies down to sleep at Bethel and then sets up the same stone as a pillar and anoints it after he has his dream of the ladder (28:11, 18, 22); he rolls the stone off the mouth of the well on his entrance into Haran (29:10); he sets up a stone pillar and pile of stones at his meeting with Laban on Mount Gilead (31:45–46); he sets up a stone pillar at Bethel once again (35:14), and then again to mark the burial place of Rachel, "the monument of the grave of Rachel until today" (35:20). We interpreted the stone on the mouth of the well and the cairn at Gilead as signifying barriers, the first between Jacob and the past—or the source to which he must return—and the second between Jacob and Laban, as well as between Jacob/Israel's new character of direct confronter of men and his old character of deceitful shadower of Esau.

In addition to these specific roles of the stones, there is a common significance shared by all the stones, and this is the function of the stone as a marker, a monument, a witness: "the monument of the grave of Rachel until today." Stones mark the place where a memorable event occurred, bearing witness of the event to those who will come later. In this sense, then, the stones, rather than being barriers against the past, are channels to it. Stones serve two functions as markers, that of marking places as well as that of marking events. When Joshua and the Israelites cross the River Jordan into Canaan they take twelve stones from the bed of the miraculously dry river, one for each tribe, and set them up at Gilgal in order to mark the crossing:

> In order that this be a sign in your midst, that when your children ask you tomorrow, What are these stones to you? You will tell them, Because the waters of the Jordan were cut off before the Ark of the Covenant of the Lord; when it passed in the Jordan the waters of the Jordan were cut off; and these stones will be a memorial for the Children of Israel forever. (Joshua 4:6–7)

The stones at Gilgal—a play on GaL, a "cairn"—are the fulfillment of Moses' earlier commandment to the Israelites in Deuteronomy 27. At the same time, however, the stones are markers of their claim to the land, a signifier of ownership that they erect as their first act on entering the land of Canaan, as they set up stones to mark military victories and other memorable events.

I would like to suggest that one of the functions of the stones that Jacob sets up at various places in Canaan is to serve as concrete reminders of the claim of the Israelites to the land of Canaan at a time when the tribes are about to be uprooted and transplanted to Egypt. It thus falls to Jacob—the patriarch of the generation that leaves Canaan and descends into the bondage of Egypt—to leave monuments of the Israelite presence in Canaan as visible and lasting links to the past occupation of the land by descendants of Abraham and Isaac.

At the same time, the markers are witnesses to the covenant between God and the Israelites, of which inheritance of the land is part (Deuteronomy 27). In the passage that records the story of Jacob's first dream at Bethel, the word for "place," MaQoM, is repeated over and over, suggesting a special connection between Jacob and the idea of place:

> Jacob left Beersheba and went to Haran. He reached a certain place [MaQoM] and went to sleep there, for the sun had set, and he took one

of the stones of the place [MaQoM] and put it at his head and lay down in that place [MaQoM]. (28:10–11)

Jacob's dream of the ladder reaching to heaven follows here; in the course of the dream, God promises to give the land on which he is lying to him and to his children, and tells him that his descendants will spread out in all directions and will be regarded by all the nations as being blessed. God's final words are a promise to return Jacob to Canaan after his sojourn in Haran:

> I am with you and I will watch over you wherever you go, and I will bring you back to this land, for I will not leave you until I have done what I have told you.
> Jacob awoke from his sleep and said, Surely the Lord is in this place [MaQoM] and I did not know. And he was afraid and said, How awesome is this place [MaQoM]; this is none other than the house of God and this is the gate of heaven.
> Jacob awoke in the morning and took the stone that he had put at his head and set it up as a pillar and anointed it with oil. And he named the place [MaQoM] Bethel ["house of God"], although Luz was the name of the city at first. (28:15–19)

Jacob, more than any of the Patriarchs, excels at naming places that will figure in later history. The names Bethel, Mahanaim, Peniel, Succot, and perhaps Gilead are all bestowed by Jacob, and all are later referred to in the accounts of the conquest of the land by Moses and Joshua.

We recall the namings that took place at the time of the Creation, when God gave names to the eternal aspects of the world—the Day and the Night, the Land and the Sea—in the first Creation account, while the names of the animals, as well as that of the woman, were given by the man in the second account. We suggested that these namings were indicative of claims to dominion. In a similar manner, then, Jacob's naming of important sites in and around Canaan may be seen as signs of his claim to these lands on behalf of his descendants— by naming the places he comes to possess them.

The role of Jacob as bearer of the promise to return to the land after the impending exile is attested also in Jacob's personal history.

God promises Jacob at two different junctures that He will return him to the land of his fathers. The first, as we saw, is the promise of the dream at Bethel, when Jacob is on his way into his first exile, into Haran. This promise is of course fulfilled after Jacob leaves his uncle Laban and survives the long-dreaded encounter with his brother Esau.

The second promise is directly related to the future exile in Egypt, since it is given when Jacob is on his way to Egypt at the invitation of Joseph and Pharaoh; this is God's last revelation in Genesis:

> And Israel and all that belonged to him made the journey, and he came to Beersheba and made sacrifices to the God of his father Isaac. God said to Israel in a vision of the night, He said, Jacob, Jacob; and he said, Here I am. He said, I am the God of your father; do not be afraid to go down to Egypt for I will make you a great nation there. I will go down with you to Egypt and I will bring you back up . . . . (46:1–4)

The promise to bring Jacob back has a twofold thrust. Since Jacob in fact dies in Egypt it seems that the promise applies to the descendants of Jacob who will return after the Exodus. This is certainly one of the meanings of the promise. However, the promise finds its fulfillment even with respect to Jacob himself, for despite the fact that he died and was embalmed in Egypt. "His sons carried him to the land of Canaan and buried him in the cave of the field of Machpelah that Abraham had bought . . . ." (50:13). The fulfillment of God's promise to return Jacob to Canaan is an assurance of God's faithfulness to his descendants as well.

Notes

1. A Midrash in Genesis Rabba (65:15), a collection compiled in the fourth or fifth century CE, connects the scapegoat with Esau and states that the sins of Jacob are carried off with the scapegoat into the wilderness.

There is a further interesting parallel to the story of Jacob and Esau in the ritual of the scapegoat on the Day of Atonement. After Jacob's final meeting with Esau at which he makes a symbolic restitution of the stolen blessing, Esau suggests that they travel together and offers to have some of his men accompany Jacob. Jacob responds by proposing that Esau go on ahead while he and his party will follow along at their own pace until they will meet up with Esau at Esau's home in Seir. Esau sets out for Seir, but Jacob goes to Succot instead, where he builds a house for himself and shelters ("succot") for his animals (33:12–17).

In the procedure for the Day of Atonement set out in the Mishna (BT *Yoma* 66b-67a), the man who takes the scapegoat out into the desert is accompanied by notables of Jerusalem who walk with him from booth to booth ("succot," prepared beforehand) until the last of the ten booths, from which he is to continue alone with the scapegoat into the desert. After pushing the scapegoat to its death, he returns to the last of the booths and remains there until the end of the Day of Atonement. The separation of the attendant from his retinue to proceed alone toward the desert, and his return to the last of the booths after leaving the scapegoat (Sa'iR) in the desert recall Jacob's separation from his brother (who is on his way to his home in Seir) and his subsequent dwelling in Succot.

David Sykes brought to my attention the significant fact that the Succot holiday ("Tabernacles") follows five days after the Day of Atonement in the Jewish calendar.

2. The injury to Jacob's hip, or more literally, "thigh-joint," may relate to a flaw that will appear in Jacob's progeny, since that is the connotation of the thigh in various places in the Hebrew Bible (for example, ". . . All the people that came to Egypt with Jacob, all his progeny"—lit. "all those who emerged from his thigh" [46:26]). A particularly appealing interpretation of this injury is that it reflects the flaw in Jacob that is the cause of the enmity among his sons, since the hostility of the ten older brothers toward Joseph is a direct consequence of Jacob's undisguised favoring of his younger son Joseph over the older ones. In other words, despite Jacob's harsh lessons at the hands of Esau and Laban, he still has not learned how destructive fraternal envy can be. Jacob's limping away from the encounter with his

adversary has an ironic relation to his renaming, for in spite of his new name meaning "straight," his walk remains crooked as a reminder that although he has changed, he remains flawed. In addition, since the wrestling with the stranger echoes the struggling of Jacob with Esau in the womb, Jacob's injured thigh may perhaps also represent retaliation for his grasping of Esau's heel.

3. That YaBoQ and VaYeABeQ play on Jacob's name was pointed out to me by David Sykes.

Interestingly, the early Greek translation of the Hebrew Bible called the Septuagint had a slightly different version of the Hebrew original, for at the end of his speech the angel says: "For you have contended with a divine being, and with men shall you prevail." According to this version, Jacob's wrestling with the angel is a precursor of his *future* prevailing over men— which can refer only to his contest with Esau, since his struggle with Laban lies in the past. This version also supports more directly our interpretation of the struggle with the angel as a dress rehearsal for Jacob's meeting with Esau.

4. The change in Jacob's name is consonant with the change in the name of the place where Jacob had his dream of the ladder in Genesis 28, where he changes the name of Luz to Bethel. Luz is from a root meaning "falsehood," and Bethel means "house of God." Similarly, Laban is called ARaMi, "Aramean" from the name of his homeland, and Jacob accuses him of deception using a word from the root RMH, "to deceive" (LaMa RiMiTaNi, "Why did you deceive me?"). ARaMi is thus a play on RaMai, "deceiver," as several Midrashim point out (Genesis Rabba 63:4, and elsewhere), also suggesting that Laban's home is a "land of deceivers."

There may perhaps be further plays on words suggesting falsehood and trickery in the account of Jacob's use of peeled rods of different kinds of wood to bring about the birth of colored and spotted sheep and goats (30:37). The three kinds of wood he chooses are LiBNe, LuZ and 'aRMoN. LiBNe suggests a connection to Laban; LuZ, as we saw, refers to "falsehood"; and 'aRMoN recalls the root 'RM, meaning "shrewdness" or "craftiness" (as in the description in Genesis 3:2 of the serpent in the Garden of Eden: "The serpent was the most cunning—'aRuM—of all the beasts of the field").

5. The Israelites are protected from the plague that destroys the Egyptian firstborn by marking their houses with the blood of the Paschal sacrifice:

Take a bundle of hyssop and dip it in the blood that is in the bowl, and touch the lintel and the two door-posts with the blood from the bowl, and let no one of you leave the door of his house until morning. The Lord will come to smite Egypt, He will see the blood on the lintel and on the two door-posts, and the Lord will skip over the door and will not allow the destroyer to enter your houses to strike. (Exodus 12:22–23)

6. Another encounter with a stranger that takes place prior to a potentially dangerous meeting of the protagonist with persons he has reason to fear appears in the story of Jacob's son Joseph; see Note 1 of the next chapter.

7. One last example of a meeting with a supernatural being in preparation for a dangerous encounter (in this case, a battle) appears in the Book of Joshua, where it serves a different function from the other instances. Immediately after the passages relating the mass circumcision of the Israelites by Joshua and the celebration of the Passover in Gilgal (see Note 9 of Chapter 8), we read the following:

When Joshua was at Jericho he looked up and saw a man standing facing him with his drawn sword in his hand; Joshua walked toward him and said to him, Are you with us or with our enemies? He said, No—I am the commander of the Lord's army; I have now come. Joshua fell on his face to the ground and prostrated himself and said to him, What does my master have to say to his servant? The commander of the Lord's army said to Joshua, Remove your shoes from your feet, for the place on which you stand is holy; and Joshua did so. (Joshua 5:13–15)

Joshua's encounter with a messenger from the Lord occurs in preparation for the siege and conquest of the well-fortified city of Jericho, Joshua's first battle as leader of the Israelites. The passage as it stands appears somewhat fragmentary, for we are not told what it is that the angel has to say to Joshua, unless God's instructions concerning the siege of Jericho—related in the following passage—are understood to have been conveyed by the Lord's commander-in-chief. Regardless of what the angel does or does not say to Joshua, however, this meeting serves several functions. First of all, it is a meeting of reassurance to Joshua that God really is on his side, although there seems to be little indication that Joshua was very apprehensive about the forthcoming battle.

Secondly, this meeting serves as a reaffirmation to Joshua, to the Israelites, and to the reader, that Joshua does indeed stand in the place of Moses as God's chosen leader. The angel's words to Joshua—"Remove your shoes from your feet, for the place on which you stand is holy"—are essentially identical to God's words to Moses at the burning bush: "Remove your shoes from your feet, for the place on which you stand is holy ground" (Exodus 3:5). As we will see in Chapter 8, this is one of several instances where Joshua's story includes a deliberate repetition of an event in the life of Moses, a repetition that has the effect of reasserting Joshua's legitimacy as the heir of Moses.

Finally, perhaps this vignette also serves as a subtle parody, since at the same time that this passage confirms Joshua's standing as Moses' replacement, it also demonstrates that Joshua is nonetheless not a Moses. Balaam, when confronted by an angel holding aloft a drawn sword, at first fails to see him at all, but when he finally does see him he realizes immediately what sort of creature he is facing. Joshua, although he has no trouble seeing the angel, does not comprehend what he sees. Whereas Balaam was blinded by his desire for wealth and honor, Joshua's vision is distorted by his personal limitations. He is not a prophet on the order of Balaam and Moses, nor is he a lawgiver and judge like Moses, but a military man who knows how to give orders and to obey them. When he sees an angel of the Lord brandishing a sword in front of him, he fearlessly walks right up to him and—blithely unaware that he is standing face to face with a supernatural being—asks him the only question that he can think of: "Are you for us or against us?" The angel, perhaps with some exasperation, has to set Joshua straight and explain to him the significance of this meeting: "No, Joshua—you're not getting it—I'm an *angel*." That possibility had not occurred to him.

CHAPTER 7

Joseph: Eyes Open, Yet Asleep

BEFORE THE CHILDREN OF ISRAEL CAN TAKE FINAL possession of the promised land of Canaan, they must first descend into the exile of Egypt. The story of Joseph and his brothers tells how they came to be in Egypt. At the same time, the story shows how God makes use of the actions of unsuspecting mortals to carry out His designs. These are the subjects of the last third of the Book of Genesis. We will see below how these themes are developed with the aid of verbal and symbolic markers for recognition, seeing, covering, and uncovering.

Communication: Words, Dreams, Interventions

A major concern of Genesis—a concern that is both explicit and implicit—is the nature of the relationship between God and human beings. This relationship takes two forms: One is the reciprocal effects of human actions on God and God's actions on humans, and the other is the narrower interaction that takes the form of communication between God and men. These two facets of the relation between the divine and the human are not distinct, since one aspect of God's role in the affairs of mankind is His communication with men, while conversely, God's participation in history is also a means of communication. Although the two kinds of interaction are tightly bound together at the beginning of the book, they gradually diverge as the narratives of Genesis develop. God continues to affect the world of men by His actions, but He communicates His intentions less and less, with the result that the events of history become progressively more opaque to its participants. There is a sharpening of the contrast between the perspectives of God and men, and the question of human awareness or ignorance of the role of God becomes more central.

The change in the relationship between God and humans is expressed in a general evolution in the way that God and human beings speak with one another. In the earliest chapters of Genesis, God and humans simply speak to one another as humans do. God tells the first man and woman to be fruitful and multiply, He tells the man which fruit he may and may not eat, and then, when the man disobeys, He rebukes him and informs him of the fate that awaits him. Some of these events take the form of dialogues, with God questioning the man and the woman and their answering Him. Thus:

> The Lord God called to the man and said to him, Where are you? He said, I heard Your sound in the garden and I was afraid because I am naked, and I hid. He said, Who told you that you are naked? Did you eat of the tree from which I had forbidden you to eat? The man said, The woman that You placed with me, she gave me of the tree, and I ate. The Lord God said to the woman, What is this that you have done? The woman said, The serpent enticed me, and I ate. (3:9–13)

This is a conversation, much like one that could have taken place between a parent and two disobedient children.

The later speech of God to Noah is one-sided. At the beginning of the story, God commands and Noah obeys, but there is no conversation. In fact, Noah says nothing at all until we are told of his curse on his youngest son and his blessing of his two other children (9:25–27). After the Flood, God blesses the survivors, lays down some rudimentary laws, and vows never again to upset the order of the world by a Flood. Once again, Noah says nothing.

When God speaks with Abraham later on, His speeches are part of an ongoing relationship with Abraham that often takes the form of extended dialogue. The closeness of God's relationship with Abraham is expressed in the rhetorical preface to God's telling him about the future destruction of Sodom and Gomorrah: "The Lord said, Will I hide from Abraham what I am doing?" (18:17). Aside from Abraham's famous negotiation with God over the fate of the wicked cities, there are several instances where real, two-sided conversations take place (for example, 15:1–9; 17:15–21; 18:13–15).

Nonetheless, a significant distancing of God from His interlocutor is evident in the formality of these dialogues. To illustrate this aspect of the conversation between God and Abraham, let us look at one of these conversations in detail:

> Abram was ninety-nine years old and the Lord showed Himself to Abram and said to him, I am El Shaddai; walk in My ways and be blameless, and I will set My covenant between Me and you and I will multiply you greatly. Abram fell on his face and God spoke to him, saying . . . . (17:1–3)
>
> God said to Abraham, Call Sarai your wife no longer Sarai, for Sarah will be her name. I will bless her and I will also give you a son of her . . . Abraham said to God, Would that Ishmael live before You . . . He finished speaking to him, and God ascended from Abraham. (17:15–22)

It is with Abraham, for the first time, that the appearances of God are announced as such—they are no longer occurrences that are a part of the natural order. The appearance of God is framed by the phrases "the Lord showed Himself to Abram" and "God ascended from Abraham," marking an event of signal importance. God's introduction of Himself by name is also new; no introduction had been necessary when He spoke to Adam or to Noah. Abraham prostrates himself when God begins to speak. Whenever Abraham speaks to God his language is highly formal, very different from the colloquial responses of Adam and Eve to God in the garden, and even further from Cain's impertinent answer to God's question about his brother Abel: "I know not; am I my brother's keeper?" Despite the frequency of God's revelations to Abraham and the intimacy of their relationship, God's appearances have become very special events. God is becoming less human and more divine, and conversely, people are becoming less divine and more human. The separation of heaven from earth that began with the Creation continues to widen.

In the subsequent appearances of God to Abraham's son Isaac, there is a further attenuation of communication between God and humans. Just as the whole of the brief account of the adventures of Isaac appears to be little more than a pale reiteration of the story of Abraham, so God's words to Isaac in His two revelations are not much more than perfunctory repetitions of the promises to his father. As we saw in our discussion of Isaac, it is clear that God's relationship with him exists only as an offshoot of God's relationship with Abraham. Furthermore, like Noah, Isaac says nothing in response to God—there is no dialogue.

People continue to speak to God, but no longer are there conversations: Isaac prays to the Lord for children and the Lord heeds his prayer (25:21), and Rebecca his wife goes "to inquire of the Lord" in a formal inquiry as to the significance of the struggling of the children in her womb (25:22). Although God continues for a time to instruct and reassure the Patriarchs and others, and although people pray to Him, after the time of Abraham there will never be another conversation in Genesis between God and a human being.

A further major change begins to take place toward the middle of the book when God first speaks to the third Patriarch, Jacob:

> Jacob left Beersheba and went to Haran. He reached a certain place and went to sleep there, for the sun had set, and he took one of the stones of the place and put it at his head and lay down in that place.
>
> He dreamt, and there was a ladder standing on the earth and its top reached heaven, and angels of God were ascending and descending it. The Lord was standing by him and said, I am the Lord, God of your father Abraham and God of Isaac; to you and to your children will I give the land that you are lying on. Your children will be as the dust of the earth, and you will spread to the west and to the east, to the north and to the south, and all the families of the earth will bless themselves by saying they would be like you and like your children. I am with you and I will watch over you wherever you go, and I will bring you back to this land, for I will not leave you until I have done what I have told you.
>
> Jacob awoke from his sleep and said, Surely the Lord is in this place and I did not know. And he was afraid and said, How awesome is this place; this is none other than the house of God and this is the gate of heaven. (28:10–17)

God does not speak to Jacob in waking reality, as He did to his fathers, but in a dream. There is more than one component to the dream, for besides hearing God speak, Jacob also sees a vision of a ladder stretching from earth to heaven, with angels ascending and descending. We learn how Jacob connects his dream to waking reality, for when he awakens he says, "Surely the Lord is in this place and I did not know."

God's first appearance to Jacob is partly veiled. Not only is this implied in the fact that the communication is in a dream, but the vision of the ladder demands interpretation. God speaks to him, but does not translate the vision explicitly. Angels of God coming and going between heaven and earth represent the constant interplay between the human world and the divine world, reassuring Jacob that he is not alone as he flees his brother's anger. His exclamation on awakening—"Surely the Lord is in this place and I did not know"—is Jacob's realization of this; he had been unaware of God's presence, but is now reassured.

The dream is self-referential: Not only does it inform Jacob of the ongoing communication between heaven and earth, but it is also *itself* a communication from heaven to earth. And it is not a unique communication, but rather a forerunner of many dreams that will follow, both to Jacob and to others. In this way it prefigures the form that subsequent communication will take. The distance between God and humanity is increasing, but only if we look for direct interaction through language; whether we are aware of it or not, the angels continue to pass back and forth. This is the theme that is developed in the continuation of the story of the sons of Jacob, which is mainly the story of Joseph.

The progressive degeneration of communication between heaven and earth continues with three pairs of dreams in the story of Joseph. Joseph himself has two dreams foretelling his future rise to greatness and ascendancy over his brothers (37:5–10); Pharaoh's deposed cupbearer and baker have dreams that Joseph correctly interprets as signifying their respective return to office and execution (40:5–22); and Pharaoh himself dreams his two famous dreams of the seven fat cows and the seven lean cows, and of the seven full ears of grain and the seven empty ears of grain—foretelling the coming seven years of plenty followed by the seven years of famine (41:1–32). All of these dreams are like the dream of Jacob in that they convey their messages through symbols. More importantly, however, they are unlike the dream of Jacob in that their manner of expression is *wholly* symbolic—God neither speaks nor appears at all. There is thus nothing explicitly divine about these dreams. Likewise, God is silent from the beginning of the story of Joseph until after the resolution that occurs near the very end of the book—when God appears in a vision of the night to Jacob to reassure him that his offspring will one day return to the land of Canaan after the exile in Egypt (46:2–4). God's last speech had occurred in His appearance to Jacob in Genesis 35, about two thirds of the way through the book. God, in Genesis, does not speak to anyone of a later generation—not even in dreams.

Nevertheless, the fact that God no longer speaks does not lead Joseph to conclude that God is therefore not present, or not concerned with what happens in the world of mortals. As Joseph tells Pharaoh before he interprets his dreams, "The dream of Pharaoh is one; God has told Pharaoh what He is about to do" (41:25), and afterward: "As for the dream appearing twice to Pharaoh, this is because the matter is set with God and God will do it quickly" (41:32).

And it is not only Joseph who must remain aware of the role of God in the events surrounding him—the text makes sure that we too do not forget it. Let us look at the description of Joseph's success in Egypt:

> Joseph was brought down to Egypt, and Potiphar, an officer of Pharaoh's, the chief steward, an Egyptian, bought him from the Ishmaelites who brought him down there. The Lord was with Joseph, and he became a successful man, and he was in the house of his Egyptian master. His master saw that the Lord was with him and that everything that he did the Lord made succeed. Joseph found favor in his eyes and he served him, and he appointed him over his household and put all he owned into his hands. From the time that he appointed him over his household and over all that he owned, the Lord blessed the household of the Egyptian because of Joseph, and the blessing of the Lord was on all that he owned in the house and in the field. (39:1–5)

Later, after having spurned the advances of Potiphar's wife and having been betrayed by her, a similar situation develops in the prison into which Joseph has been thrown:

> Joseph's master took him and put him into the prison, into the place where the prisoners of the king were jailed, and he was there in the prison. The Lord was with Joseph and was kind to him, and He made him find favor in the eyes of the keeper of the prison. The keeper of the prison put all the prisoners in the prison into Joseph's charge, and everything that there was to be done there he would do. The keeper of the prison did not supervise

anything that he did as the Lord was with him, and whatever he did the Lord made succeed. (39:20–23)

The Lord is with Joseph no matter where he is. God's providence is apparent in the favor that Joseph finds in the eyes of all his beholders. From being the favored son of his father Jacob, he becomes the favorite of Potiphar, desired by Potiphar's wife, then the favorite of the keeper of the prison, until he finally wins the favor of Pharaoh himself and becomes second only to the king in all the land of Egypt. But despite the fact that God's providence is everywhere said to be responsible for Joseph's success, there is a total absence of explicit divine instruction and intervention throughout the story of Joseph.

Divine Concealment

Genesis 37 begins with the description of Jacob's special relationship with the son of his favorite wife—Joseph, the son of Rachel— and of Joseph's and Jacob's remarkable insensitivity to the feelings of the other brothers. Joseph bears tales of the brothers' misdeeds to their father, who loves him more than all of his other sons. Jacob presents Joseph with a special ornamented coat (the famous "coat of many colors"), further fueling their resentment. If these were not already reasons enough to make them hate him, Joseph eagerly tells his brothers his transparently symbolic dreams of their future subservience and obeisance to him.

If Joseph had been more sensitive to his brothers, or at least more diplomatic, perhaps he would have been spared his abduction and sale by them, and the story would have had to reach its foreordained conclusion in some other way—but this was not to be the way the story unfolds. When the brothers have the chance, they tear Joseph's coat from him and throw him into a pit from which he is later pulled and sold into slavery in Egypt for twenty pieces of silver.[1] There, by his successful interpretation of the dreams of Pharaoh, and by his sagacious advice to store up grain during the years of plenty, he becomes the viceroy of Egypt and saves both the Egyptians and his family from the famine foretold in the dreams.

The famine forces Joseph's brothers to go down to Egypt to buy provisions. Since Joseph is the one in charge of dispensing food, they must approach him and bow down to him, but fail to recognize who he is. Joseph, however, recognizes his brothers. At first he conceals his identity from them, and then, when he finally reveals himself, he says:

> Come close to me, and they came close, and he said, I am your brother Joseph whom you sold to Egypt. Now, do not be sorrowful and do not be distressed that you sold me here, for God sent me here before you to save life. For the famine has already been in the land for two years, and there will be five more years without plowing or reaping. God sent me ahead of you so that you would survive in the land and to save your lives in a great deliverance. Now it was not you who sent me here but God, and He has made me a chief to Pharaoh and master of all his household and ruler over all the land of Egypt. Hurry and go up to my father and say to him, Thus says your son Joseph, God has made me master of all Egypt; come down to me, do not tarry. (45:4–9)

The resolution of the story of Joseph's tribulations in Egypt comes with the revelation that earlier events had been part of a hidden providential plan to ensure the survival of the house of Jacob. This revelation comes to the actors in a drama of which they had been unaware. In addition, we, the readers, see in the drama a step toward the fulfillment of the prophecy to Abraham in 15:13, when God told him of the future exile and enslavement in Egypt.

The ignorance of the protagonists allows the text to play ironically with the events transpiring around them in a way that takes the reader into its confidence, as it were. For example, when Joseph demands to see their youngest brother, who has been left behind in Canaan, the brothers' feeling of guilt over the sale of Joseph surfaces: Why is the Egyptian so harsh to them? "But we are to blame, for our brother, that we saw his distress when he pleaded with us and we did not listen; this is why this trouble has come to us" (42:21). They are right, of course, but we know much better than they how true their words are.

Before Joseph allows the brothers to return to Canaan with the grain that they have purchased from him, he compels them to leave their brother Simeon[2] hostage in Egypt to ensure their return with their youngest brother, Benjamin. Joseph sends them on their way, but secretly returns the money that they had paid for the food. When they discover the money in their sacks they marvel, "What is this that God has done to us?" (42:28). This is the question that reigns over all of the story of Joseph; we also know the answer in a way that the brothers themselves will not until they have been tested further.

There is a further irony in the return of the money to the brothers. The money that they had paid to Joseph for the grain has become a symbolic restitution of the money that they had received for his sale to the passing traders. But the restitution is not accepted, and they must go home with their money while leaving their brother Simeon imprisoned in Egypt—just as had happened years earlier when they went home without Joseph, but in possession of the money for which they had sold him into slavery. When they return to Egypt bringing Benjamin with them, they attempt to return the money to Joseph, but he again has it put back into their sacks, and now threatens to keep Benjamin prisoner in Egypt (44:1–17). The brothers wish to leave the money and to take home their captive brothers, but Joseph will return the money and will keep their brothers. The money shuttling back and forth between Canaan and Egypt is the money of the sale of Joseph. There can be no final resolution and forgiveness until the brothers demonstrate their willingness to fulfill their brotherly responsibility to one another. This is achieved only when they offer themselves as slaves when Joseph threatens to keep Benjamin—and especially when Judah offers to take the place of Benjamin as Joseph's prisoner in order to spare their father more grief (44:9, 16, 33). The money floats in limbo until the question of the brotherliness of the brothers has been resolved.

Some of the other ironies are subtler, making use of elements of earlier narratives that were revelatory of the personalities of the actors. The conciliatory character of the Patriarch Jacob is introduced into the account of the brothers' conflict with the Egyptian viceroy in Genesis 43, when the brothers attempt to persuade their father to allow them to take Benjamin with them on their second trip to Egypt, as Joseph has demanded. For, as the brothers had put it, the man had told them that they would not be permitted to "see his face" unless they brought their youngest brother with them, an allusion to the theme of recognition and ignorance:

> Israel their father said to them, If it be so, then do this: Take of the pro-
> duce of the land in your containers and take a gift [MiNḤa] to the man,
> some balm, and some honey, gum and laudanum, nuts and almonds. And
> take double money with you; the money that was returned in your sacks
> take back, it might be an error. (43:11–12)

When the brothers return to Egypt, Joseph's representative does not accept their money. They subsequently present Joseph with the gift: "Joseph came into the house and they brought him the gift that they had into the house, and they bowed to him down to the ground" (43:26). In this and their earlier bowing to Joseph (Genesis 42) we are of course reminded of Joseph's adolescent dreams of his brothers' obeisance (Genesis 37). But this is not the only thing that comes to mind; the gift brought to appease a powerful and threatening brother whose "face" is to be seen has appeared before—in the meeting of Jacob and Esau, as Jacob prepared to meet the brother whom he had tricked out of his birthright and blessing.

Jacob, in great trepidation over his imminent face-to-face en-counter with his wronged and powerful and, apparently, threaten-ing brother, attempted to assuage his presumed wrath with a gift (MiNḤa). Esau at first graciously declined the gift, but Jacob con-tinued to press it on him until he accepted it. Restitution was thus effected at the meeting that is described as "seeing the face" (see Chapter 6). There is a parallel here to the gift that the brothers bring to Joseph at Jacob's suggestion, although the fact that Joseph does not accept their money makes it clear that the wrong has yet to be redressed. In addition to the returned money, the gifts brought by Joseph's brothers also recall the sale of Joseph—for the Ishmaelites who took him down to Egypt as a slave were also carrying a load of gum and balm and laudanum bound for Egypt (37:25).

The story of Joseph is the culmination of the Book of Genesis, returning us to concerns that we first raised in the two accounts of the Creation at the beginning of the book. We saw there that the universe of the Creation can be approached from two perspectives—that of

God and that of man—and that the perspective of God is accessible to us in only a limited way. The protagonists in the story of Joseph move about in the dark for the most part, and although their dreams are revelations in an important sense, the revelations are obscure in that they convey their messages symbolically, and are often not understood by the dreamers without help. God's concealment is evident in the way that the characters participate in the events that transpire around them without being aware of the significance of those events or of their own actions.

These two aspects of hiddenness—in communication and in actions—are emblematic of the concealment of the divine from the human, and are expressions of the distance between God and humans that has been growing since the beginning of the book. But this concealment is not impenetrable, because both dreams and waking reality lend themselves to interpretation. Just as Joseph interprets the messages of the dreams as they relate to the events of the story, so must the events themselves be interpreted—ultimately revealing hitherto-unsuspected significance. The story as a whole is an affirmation that God participates in human affairs, no matter how hidden His role. It remains incumbent on us to be aware of this role by understanding history as a linked and meaningful chain of events rather than as a series of occurrences ruled by nothing more than caprice.

Human Concealment

Parallel to the divine concealment in the story of Joseph is the concealment that goes on among the protagonists themselves. Joseph's brothers conceal their treachery from their father Jacob; Pothiphar's wife conceals her attempted seduction of Joseph from her husband, and deceives him with a self-serving account that makes Joseph the seducer; Joseph conceals his identity from his brothers when they come to him to buy grain to relieve the hunger in their households; Joseph surreptitiously returns the money that his brothers bring in payment; Joseph conceals his silver goblet in the sack of his brother Benjamin in order to have the brothers brought back and tested further.

The major motif in the narrative is that of recognition. Jacob is asked to recognize the bloody coat of his son; Joseph recognizes his brothers when they come to him in Egypt, while they do not recognize him; less literally, the brothers fail to recognize the fraternity that binds them to Joseph, and the filial respect they owe their father. There are word plays on terms for conspiring, recognition, and dissimulation or estrangement. And indeed, the evolution of perception and recognition in the story of Joseph parallels the maturation that both Joseph and his brothers—represented primarily by Judah, as we will see—undergo.

Word plays involving recognition and estrangement are developed through a sequence of verbs that, in effect, signal the development of the brothers throughout the story. The first in the series appears when the brothers plot to kill Joseph when they see him approaching from afar—VaYiTNaKLu, from the root NKL, "to conspire." The next is Judah's suggestion that, rather than murdering Joseph, he be sold:

> What good will it do us if we kill our brother and cover his blood? Let us sell him to the Ishmaelites. (37:26–27)

"Let us sell him" in Hebrew is LêKu VêNiMKêReNu, the second word from the root MKR, "to sell." When the brothers bring Joseph's torn and bloody coat to Jacob in order to mislead him, they say:

> This have we found, look at it [lit. "recognize," HaKeR Na], is this the coat of your son or not? He recognized it [VaYaKiRa] and said, It is my son's coat. A wild beast has eaten him; Joseph has fallen prey. (37:32–33)

The relevant root here is NKR, "to recognize," and the recognition has a double sense—for it is also a call for Jacob to recognize his own responsibility for the brothers' hostility to Joseph. In the immediately succeeding narrative of Judah and Tamar (which we will discuss shortly), Tamar too challenges Judah to "recognize," and the recognition to which Judah is forced is also twofold. He must acknowledge his betrayal of his brother and his father as well as his misleading of Tamar:

> Recognize [HaKeR Na], to whom belong this seal and cord and staff . . .
> Judah recognized [them] [VaYaKeR] and said, She is more in the right
> than I . . . . (38:25–26)

Not only is this the same root, NKR, but the challenge to "recognize," HaKeR Na, is exactly what the brothers had said to Jacob to mislead him about Joseph's fate. As the story unfolds, years later the brothers make their way down to Joseph, now viceroy in Egypt, to buy grain:

> He recognized them [VaYaKiReM], but behaved as a stranger to them [VaYiTNaKeR][3] ... Joseph recognized [VaYaKeR] his brothers, but they did not recognize him [Lo HiKiRuHu]. (42:7–8)

There is a play here on two senses of the root NKR, "to recognize" and "to be strange or foreign."

The final word play in the sequence occurs near the climax and resolution of the test to which Joseph has been subjecting his brothers, when he sees his youngest brother, Benjamin:

> ... for his pity on his brother was aroused [NiKMêRu, lit. "warmed"] and he had to weep, and he went inside and wept there. (43:30)

The root KMR—contrasting with all the previous verbal signposts that were conveyed with similar roots—marks the beginning of the resolution of the estrangement between Joseph and his brothers. The betrayal, the recognition and the lack of recognition, the dissimulation—all begin to dissolve in Joseph's feelings for his younger brother, and he cannot keep from acting as a brother for much longer.[4] Here too, as we saw in the stories of the Flood and of Jacob, the last word play in the series signals forgiveness and reconciliation.

The story of Joseph revolves around failures of perception. Jacob fails to see how his favoring of one of his sons fosters hatred among the brothers; Joseph's insensitivity prevents him from seeing that his brothers' already smoldering envy can only be inflamed by his telling them the dreams of their future obeisance to him; the brothers let their envy of Joseph blind them to their fraternal obligation to him, as well as to the great pain they will cause their father by doing away with his favorite. These failures of perception are the driving forces in the history. Human blindness to the consequences of human actions is thus a concomitant of divine hiddenness—and might perhaps contribute to the divine concealment—since, as we will see, human concealment and blindness accompany the hiding of God even before the story of Joseph.

Clothing and Betrayal I

In keeping with the themes of concealment and failures of perception, the central image in the story of Joseph is that of clothing—both as a means of disguise and concealment and as emblematic of the disparity between what is externally visible and the truth that underlies it. The themes of deception and disguise were introduced when Jacob disguised himself as his older brother Esau in order to receive a blessing intended for the firstborn. At the instigation of his mother Rebecca, Jacob put on Esau's clothing and covered his arms and neck with goatskins in order to pass himself off as the more hirsute Esau before his blind old father. As a result of this deception, Isaac bestowed on him the blessing that he had intended for Esau (Genesis 27). This episode foreshadows the deceptions that follow in the story of Joseph.

Prior to Jacob's disguise, clothing had figured significantly in only three connections—all having to do with knowledge or the lack of it. The first is the story of Adam and Eve in the Garden, when they made themselves garments of fig leaves after eating the fruit of the Tree of Knowledge and awakening to their nakedness (3:7). After their rebuke by God, He Himself supplied them with tunics of skin to cover themselves (3:21). The second instance is also related to the covering of nakedness, this time that of the drunken Noah by his sons Shem and Japhet, in a story that is a transformation of the earlier Tree of Knowledge episode in the Garden of Eden (9:20–23; see Chapter 4, "Erasing the World"). Clothing is essentially absent from the next fourteen chapters (although clothes are mentioned among the gifts that Abraham's servant gives Rebecca in Genesis 24; it is not clear if this has any special significance) until it is reintroduced when Rebecca covers herself from her future husband, Isaac, before their first meeting:

> Rebecca looked up and saw Isaac and fell from the camel. She said to the servant, Who is that man walking in the field toward us? The servant said, He is my master. She took the veil and covered herself. (24:64–65)

It is Rebecca who later clothes Jacob in Esau's garments and covers him with goatskins in order to deceive Isaac. These last incidents pave the way for the uses of clothing in what follows.

When we come to the story of Joseph there is clothing and unclothing everywhere. Jacob gives Joseph the ornamented coat that his brothers tear from him and dip in blood to imply Joseph's death by wild beast (37:31–33); Potiphar's wife snatches Joseph's garment from him and displays it to her husband to support her seduction story (39:16–18); when Joseph is released from the prison and brought to Pharaoh, he changes his clothing (41:14); after interpreting Pharaoh's dreams, Joseph is given royal garments of fine linen (41:42); after revealing himself to his brothers, he gives them gifts of "changes of clothing" (45:22); and at various appropriate places in the narrative, people rend their garments (when Reuben comes to look for Joseph in the pit and finds that he is no longer there (37:29); when Jacob sees Joseph's bloody coat (37:34); when Joseph's stolen goblet of silver is found in Benjamin's sack (44:13)—nowhere else in Genesis are garments rent). In addition, when Joseph accuses his brothers of being spies, he charges them with coming "to see the nakedness of the land" (42:9, 12).

Judah and His Sons: Tamar's Revelation

A particularly revealing episode embedded in the Joseph narrative is the story of Judah and Tamar, to which we have already alluded several times. Here we will review this story and discuss in detail its place within the main story line about Joseph and his brothers, and see how it addresses and illuminates the underlying concerns of the narrative.

Genesis 38—in which the events that befall Judah are recounted—appears as a strange digression that interrupts the story of the adventures of Joseph. We read that after the abduction and sale of Joseph, Judah parts from his brothers and marries a Canaanite woman by whom he has three sons—Er, Onan, and Shela. Judah takes a wife named Tamar for his eldest son. However, "Er, Judah's firstborn son, was evil in the eyes of the Lord, and the Lord killed him" (38:7). Because Er has died childless, Judah tells his next son, Onan, to perform the fraternal duty of the levirate by marrying Tamar in order that their offspring may perpetuate the name of the dead brother:

> Judah said to Onan, Cohabit with your brother's wife and perform the levirate marriage with her in order to perpetuate the seed of your brother. But Onan knew that the seed would not be his, and whenever he cohabited with his brother's wife he wasted it [the seed] on the ground in order not to give seed to his brother. What he did was evil in the eyes of the Lord, and He killed him too. (38:8–10)

After the death of Onan, a redoubled obligation to marry Tamar falls on Judah's youngest son, Shela. Fearful that a fate like that of his brothers will befall Shela if he marries Tamar, Judah promises Tamar that Shela will marry her—but puts her off with the excuse that Shela is still too young, and tells her to wait. Time passes, Judah's wife dies, and Shela grows up. When Tamar sees that Judah is still withholding Shela from her, she takes matters into her own hands:

> Tamar was told, Your father-in-law is going up to Timna to shear his sheep.[5] She took off her widow's garments and covered herself with a veil and wrapped herself, and sat at the entrance to the double wells on the road to Timna, for she saw that Shela was grown and she had not been given to him as a wife.
> Judah saw her and thought she was a harlot, because she had covered her face. He went off to her to the road and said, Come let me lie with you, for he did not know that she was his daughter-in-law. She said, What will you give me for lying with me? He said, I will send a goat-kid from the flocks; and she said, If you leave a pledge until you send it. He said, What pledge shall I give you? She said, Your seal and your cord and your staff in your hand. He gave them to her and lay with her, and she conceived by him.
> She arose and went away, and took off her veil and put on her widow's garments. (38:13–19)

Tamar exchanges her widow's garments for a veil with which she covers her face; once she has accomplished her purpose, she re-dons her widow's garb and waits.

When Judah later sends the kid to fulfill his pledge, Tamar is nowhere to be found, and the locals maintain that there had never been a harlot at the place of the encounter. Three months later, Tamar's pregnancy becomes apparent and Judah is informed of her "harlotry."

He orders her to be taken out and burnt. She sends the seal, cord, and staff to him and says:

> . . . I am pregnant by the man to whom these belong; she said, Recognize [HaKeR Na], to whom belong this seal and cord and staff? Judah recognized [them] [VaYaKeR] and said, She is more in the right than I, for I did not give her to my son Shela; and he did not know her again. (38:25–26)

Tamar gives birth to twin boys, whose birth recalls that of the brothers Jacob and Esau; one of these twins is the ancestor of the royal Davidic line.

It is Judah who bears the primary responsibility for the sale of Joseph. Before the sale, Reuben, the eldest of the brothers, attempts to rescue Joseph by persuading the others to throw him into a pit and not to kill him right away. While Joseph is in the pit awaiting the decision concerning his final disposition by the brothers, we read:

> They sat down to eat . . . Judah said to his brothers, What good will it do us if we kill our brother and cover his blood? (37:25–26)

The brothers have sat down to a meal; their passion is presumably cooling as they begin to deliberate about what to do with Joseph. Judah then begins his speech by arguing against murdering him—he calls him "our brother"—and we are led to expect that he will exhort the brothers to release the boy and send him home. But, once he has the ear of the brothers, he does no such thing. Instead he says, "Let us sell him to the Ishmaelites and let not our hand do him harm" (37:27). When it was apparently in Judah's power to save Joseph, he instead sealed his fate.

Judah's role in the sale of Joseph is the reason for Judah's loss of his own sons and his humiliating deception by his daughter in-law. First his eldest son Er dies, and then, as a result of a lack of fraternal feeling, his second son also dies. The repetition of the word "brother" four times in the passage dealing with Onan's refusal to perpetuate his brother's line (se above) leaves little room for doubt about his sin: His death is the result of his failure to perform his fraternal obligation. All Judah can do now is try to protect his last remaining son, Shela, by preventing his marriage to Tamar. Judah thus experiences firsthand the consequences of discord among one's children.

Later on, when the brothers finally prevail on Jacob to send Benjamin down to Egypt with them as the cruel viceroy has demanded, we understand why only the words of Judah carry sufficient weight to convince the old man to permit his youngest to go. First it is Reuben who tries to persuade Jacob, but to no avail:

> Reuben said to his father, Kill my two sons if I do not bring him to you; entrust him to me and I will return him to you. He said, My son will not go down with you . . . . (42:37–38)

When Reuben—who had already before proved ineffectual in protecting Joseph—speaks to Jacob about killing his two sons, Jacob's lack of trust in him is only strengthened: Reuben's words make it clear that he does not understand the grief of a bereaved father, who now dreads the loss of yet another son. On the other hand, when Judah—who has actually suffered the loss that Reuben's empty words advert to, and who was himself faced with the possibility of losing *his* youngest son—offers his assurance that he will bring the boy back, Jacob accepts his offer (43:8–14).

Judah's bitter experience with his own sons also explains why it is his plea to Joseph for the liberty of Benjamin that causes Joseph to break down and reveal himself to his brothers. In Judah's speech to Joseph, it is the elder son's sympathy for their old father that finally undoes Joseph's tightly controlled masquerade:

> Judah approached him and said, Please, my lord . . . We said to my lord, We have an old father and a child of his old age whose brother is dead, and he alone is left of his mother, and his father loves him . . . And we said to my lord, The boy cannot leave his father, for if he leaves his father he will die . . . Your servant, my father, said to us, You know that my wife bore me two sons, and one left me and I believe that he was killed by a beast and I have not seen him again. And if you take this one too from me and disaster befalls him, you will cause me to die a sorrowful death . . . So how can I go up to my father without bringing the boy, lest I witness the evil that will befall my father. And Joseph could not restrain himself . . . . (44:18–45:1)

Judah's plea is not so much for Benjamin as it is for Jacob, whose sorrow he understands as none of the others can; the repetition of the word "father" more than ten times in the original passage bespeaks his concern and has the effect of finally breaking through to Joseph.

There are many things that strike the reader—especially the reader of the original Hebrew—in the story of Judah and Tamar. We have seen how the story relates the experience of Judah to the suffering of Jacob over the enmity among his sons. Tamar's deception of Judah by changing her clothing is crucial to the narrative and hearkens back to Joseph's bloody coat with which the brothers deceived Jacob, as well as to Esau's clothing with which Jacob disguised himself. The kid that Judah promises to Tamar, but which never reaches her, recalls the goat whose blood represented the blood of Joseph and the goatskins that covered Jacob's arms when he deceived Isaac. Moreover, the shock that Judah felt when he was confronted with the evidence of his own responsibility for Tamar's pregnancy would have been magnified by the simultaneous accusation of his crime against his brother and his father that is implicit in Tamar's challenge. When she shows him the seal, the cord, and the staff that he had left as collateral for the kid, she says "Recognize—HaKeR Na," the very words that he and his brothers had used when they brought the bloody coat of Joseph to Jacob: "Recognize—HaKeR Na—is this the coat of your son or not?" (37:32). And just as "HaKeR Na" was more than simply a request to identify a garment when spoken to Jacob—but also a call to recognize his own responsibility—so Tamar's "HaKeR Na" has a meaning that goes beyond the cord, the seal, and the staff that she shows Judah.

And perhaps most remarkable of all is the name of the place where Tamar waits to entice Judah, the place that I have translated as "the entrance to the double wells," PeTaH 'eNaYiM in Hebrew. Others have translated this expression in a number of different ways, but no matter which turns out to be the most literally correct, the Hebrew expression is a striking word play: The words are also translatable as "the opening of the eyes." These two Hebrew words tell us unambiguously what the story of Judah and Tamar—and the story of Joseph—is all about.

And if the intent of the story of Judah and Tamar were not clear enough, the text also helps us along by presenting numerous plays on the names in the story. The first relates to Er, the oldest son of Judah, whose name is related to the root meaning "childless" and is at the same time an inversion of R'a, "evil" ("'ER, Judah's firstborn son, was evil in the eyes of the Lord, and the Lord killed him"). The name of the second son, Onan, plays on a root that means "bereavement." The last son's name, Shela, plays on the root that means "to delude," as when the Shunamite woman promised a son by the prophet Elisha in II Kings (4:28) begs him not to delude her with false hope, using a word with the same root. Judah's promise of Shela to Tamar was never intended to be kept and was made only to mislead her. The name of the place where Judah's sons are born, KêZiB, refers to a root that means "falsehood" or "disappointment." And finally, the name Judah plays on the root meaning "to confess" or "to acknowledge."

The most suggestive of all the names is that of Tamar herself, which is a play on the word TêMuRa—meaning "exchange" or "substitution," and in an extended sense, "retribution." Thus, Onan is obligated to substitute for the dead Er in marrying Tamar, as Shela is later bound to substitute for both his brothers. Tamar, in disguising herself, substitutes a harlot for the daughter-in-law of Judah, and in doing so causes Judah himself to take the place of his son Shela in impregnating her. It thus happens that Judah, in preventing the fulfillment of the levirate obligation by Shela, becomes himself the one to fulfill the duty. At the same time, Judah suffers retribution for the pain he had caused his father by being placed in a similar situation and losing sons as a result of fraternal discord. The final substitution occurs in the birth of the twin sons of Tamar and Judah at the end of the episode, when the younger brother bursts forth to take the presumptive firstborn's place—an episode that refers to the story of Jacob and Esau, as we saw in our discussion of the story of Jacob in our previous chapter.[6,7]

Clothing and Betrayal II

There is an evolution in the function of clothing in Genesis. In the earliest uses of clothing, in the stories of Adam and Eve and of Noah, the garment serves the simple function of covering nakedness, although in both instances clothing is already related to knowledge—the Tree of Knowledge and Noah's loss of self-awareness. But there is no imputation of any intent to mislead by covering oneself. Rebecca's covering herself with the veil when she first meets her future husband Isaac is a covering of herself *from* Isaac; this is a role that she continues to play through her son Jacob. When Rebecca covers Jacob with goatskins and dresses him in Esau's clothes, the goal is to disguise the wearer as someone else—to make Isaac think that his younger son is really his older son. Disguise is the purpose of Tamar also when she takes off her widow's garments and covers herself with a veil to mislead Judah into thinking that she is a harlot. With Jacob and Tamar, the attention of the victims of the deception is directed away from the person behind the clothing to the clothing itself. From simple covering, clothing has become disguise.

In the story of Joseph, clothing continues to serve the same two functions—(mis)representation and betrayal. Joseph's ornamented coat is the sign of the favoritism his father shows him, and also of the special destiny that awaits him. The brothers' tearing the coat and dipping it into goat's blood to make their father believe that Joseph has been killed by a wild animal is part and parcel of their betrayal of their brother, and of their father; at the same time it recalls the goatskins that Jacob had used to deceive *his* father in the competition with *his* brother. What is more, the garment takes on a life of its own in this episode: It no longer functions to clothe someone, but is rather used as evidence that Joseph has been torn by a wild beast. In Egypt, Joseph's garment, left behind in the hands of Potiphar's wife, is similarly an instrument of betrayal—it is his mistress' evidence that he tried to seduce her. Once again, clothing stands for the person, in the absence of any wearer at all. The word repeatedly used for the garment in the episode of Potiphar's wife is BeGeD, a play on another meaning of the identical root—"betrayal, faithlessness."

People are identified and understood by means of their clothing, illustrating in a concrete way how perceptions in the story are determined by external appearance. Changes of clothing—those of Jacob, Joseph, Tamar, and Joseph's brothers (who are given gifts of "changes of clothing" by Joseph)—serve not only to mislead, but also to point to significant changes in the underlying persons, whether in their role or in their fortune. We the readers, as well as the protagonists, understand the evolution of the characters in part by their clothes. This approach to reality stops at surfaces, seeing not the inner person but the external garment. This is the reality that the protagonists see—they have no way to penetrate to the underlying essence. The blindness that had at one time been specific to Isaac, who could not see Jacob through Esau's clothing, has become a general affliction.

Clothing, like a symbol, occludes understanding at the same time as it fosters it. In this way, all clothing—and every symbol as well—betrays. Symbols appear not only in the dreams that the characters must interpret, but also in the events that transpire around them. The symbols are misinterpreted by those to whom they are displayed; we have seen this in the brothers' use of Joseph's coat to deceive Jacob and in Joseph's betrayal by Potiphar's wife using his tunic. At the end of the story of Judah and Tamar we are told of the struggle between the twin sons of Tamar that takes place at the time of their birth:

> While she was giving birth he put out his hand, and the midwife took a red thread [ŠaNi] and tied it on his hand to signify: This one came out first [RIŠoNa]. But as he pulled his hand back, his brother emerged . . . .
> (38:28–29)

The red thread, the ŠaNi, had been intended to signal priority, but the real significance of the thread turns out to be exactly the opposite, for ŠaNi in reality points to the word that means "second"—ŠeNi.

The larger misperception—that history is determined solely by human actions—is not corrected until the final revelation near the end of the book. As Joseph says to his brothers, "Now it was not you who sent me here, but God" (45:8). And later still, when the brothers fear Joseph's revenge after Jacob's death:

> Joseph said to them, Do not be afraid, for can I take the place of God? You intended it for evil for me, but God intended it for good. (50:19–20)

The symbols do not function as symbols only for the actors in the drama, however; they serve as symbols for the reader also. And just as the characters in the story must interpret the symbols, so must the reader of the story interpret the symbols in order to interpret the story. There are messages that the text transmits to the reader—as messages are sent to Jacob, to Joseph, and to others in the story. Although we as readers enjoy the advantage of knowing what the story is about before the characters do, the messages to the reader too are often subtle, hidden in word plays, or in significant repetitions, or even in symbols, like the clothing that serves in the story of Joseph as a symbol—the symbol of a symbol.

Paradigms

Let us turn to what has by now become obvious: The narratives of Genesis incorporate paradigmatic themes and symbols that run from the very beginning of the book to its very end. We saw earlier that paradigms introduced in the Garden of Eden story are played on and transformed in the story of Noah and the vineyard, the Sodom narrative (especially the story of Lot and his daughters), the bringing home of Rebecca as a wife for Isaac, the deception of Isaac by Jacob at Rebecca's instigation, the misleading of Jacob by his sons with the aid of the bloody ornamented tunic, and the story of Judah and Tamar. Thus, for example, it is Isaac's blindness that occasions his deception by his son Jacob acting in collaboration with his wife Rebecca—achieved with the help of some clothing and goatskins. We have here the same constellation that appears in the Tree of Knowledge story: blindness, ignorance, knowledge, and clothing. The curse that ends God's rebuke to Adam and his wife ("Cursed be the earth . . . By the sweat of your brow . . . In pain will you bear children") is carried over into Jacob's fear that if he goes ahead with his mother's scheme he will bring on himself a curse rather than a blessing, and in his mother's reply that she will take the curse on herself (27:12–13). In the story of Noah and the vineyard we find a similar constellation, including a curse on the youngest son; likewise in the story of Sodom and its wickedness and the escape of Lot and his daughters—although this story differs from the others in the absence of an explicit curse on the Moabites and Ammonites, who will nevertheless remain permanently excluded from intermingling with the Israelites (Deuteronomy 23:4–7).

We also see variations on the paradigm. There are two varieties of betrayal, that of a father by his children, and that of a man by a woman. The misleading of Jacob by his sons who show him the bloodied coat of Joseph is an example of the former paradigm, as is the betrayal of Noah by his son Ham—who did *not* cover him with the garment; the story of Judah and Tamar is an instance of the latter. In the story of Lot and his daughters there is a conflation of the two sub-paradigms—the daughters are at the same time Lot's children and his sexual partners—as there is in the deception of Isaac by his son and his wife acting in concert. The deception of Judah by Tamar with the veil is also a combination of the two sub-paradigms: She is both the wife of Judah's dead sons as well as the mother of his new sons. The two most intimate human relationships are depicted through the disjunct perceptions of the members of the relationship. A man can be deceived by his wife and his children, as he can also have his eyes opened by them—sometimes at one and the same time.

We might ask why it is that no woman is ever successfully deceived by a man. The answer to this question reveals what it is that lies at the root of all the deceptions in all the stories. The coverings and hidings and deceptions that occur in Genesis are strategies used by the less powerful member in an intimate family relationship to assert his—or more often, her—will in a conflict of aims with a more powerful member. In general, this means that wives will deceive husbands and that children will deceive fathers, since the stringency of the rules governing interactions within the ancient Near Eastern family would preclude a direct confrontation. Likewise, the very first instance of hiding and covering occurs in the Garden of Eden, where it is the man who hides from the God Whom he surely cannot confront openly.

This "sociological" interpretation of the deception paradigm also makes it immediately obvious why it is that the conflicts between siblings take a form that is so different from the other conflicts. The reason is simply that the sibling relationship is one of parity, more or less, and conflicts can therefore be played out openly. Horrible as it may be for Cain to murder Abel and for Joseph's brothers to conspire to kill him, the idea that a son or a wife might murder a father or a husband—or sell him into slavery—is too egregious to entertain seriously at all. By contrast, fraternal conflicts—rooted in envy and competition—differ from the kinds of discord that can color filial or marital relationships, and are expressed with a directness that would not be possible in the other cases. Thus it is that the third intimate relationship—that among siblings—is fraught with conflict even to the point of murder.

This brings us to another paradigmatic pattern that pervades the Book of Genesis. As we saw in the preceding chapter, there is a joining of the theme of the competition between the older and the younger child—and, in some of the cases, loss of a younger son—with those of blindness and deception. The paradigm begins with the competition for God's favor between Cain and Abel, both of whom bring offerings (4:3–12). Despite the fact that Cain, the elder, is the one who initiates the offerings, his is rejected while Abel's is accepted. Cain, in consternation at God's favoring his younger brother, rises up and murders Abel and then impudently lies to God to hide his crime.

There is a parallel in the competition between Jacob and Esau: Isaac asks his firstborn son Esau to go out hunting and to prepare for him a meal of game, but the younger Jacob slips in before his brother can return and offers his father a meal that Isaac eats. Esau determines to murder his brother, but their mother Rebecca saves Jacob by having him sent away to her brother Laban.

When God confronted Cain, he attempted to evade responsibility with an impertinent response: "Am I my brother's keeper?" God answered:

> What have you done? Your brother's blood cries out to Me from the earth. And now, be accursed from the earth which has opened up its mouth to take your brother's blood from your hands. (4:10–11)

The blood of Abel crying out from the earth is evoked in the casting of Joseph into the pit in the earth by his older brothers, driven mad with envy by Joseph's favored treatment by their father.

The paradigm of competition, deception, and supplanting of the older by the younger sibling continues with Rebecca's and Jacob's tricking of the blind Isaac. These themes are played upon in the irony of Jacob's expiation at the hands of Laban. After agreeing to give Jacob his younger daughter Rachel in return for Jacob's seven years of labor, Laban substitutes his elder daughter Leah for Rachel on the wedding night. In the story of Tamar, the deception of Judah leads to the birth of a pair of twins who, like Jacob and Esau, fight to be the firstborn at the moment of their birth.

Practically every case of fraternity in Genesis, starting with the very first pair of brothers—Cain and Abel—is a situation of conflict.

There are more examples: When the shepherds of Abraham and Lot quarrel, Abraham says, "Let there be no quarrel between us . . . for we are men who are brothers" (13:8); when the townspeople of Sodom attack Lot he says: "Do not do evil, my brothers" (19:7); Judah's son Onan, who refuses to perpetuate his brother's name (38:9).

There is a remarkable ironic reversal of the paradigm of deception and fraternal competition in the account of Jacob's blessing of his two grandsons before his death:

> Israel saw the sons of Joseph and said, Who are these? Joseph said to his father, They are my sons, whom God has given me here. He said, Bring them to me and I will bless them. Israel's eyes were dim with age—he could not see—and he brought them near to him, and he kissed them and embraced them . . .
>
> Joseph took the two of them, Ephraim in his right hand to the left of Israel, and Menashe in his left hand to the right of Israel, and he brought them near to him. Israel stretched out his right hand and placed it on Ephraim's head—he was the younger—and his left hand on Menashe's head; he crossed his hands, although Menashe was the firstborn . . . Joseph saw that his father had placed his right hand on Ephraim's head, and he was displeased, and he tried to lift his father's hand to move it from Ephraim's head to Menashe's head. Joseph said to his father, Not so, my father, for this one is the firstborn, put your right hand on his head. His father demurred, and said, I know, my son, I know; he too will become a nation, and he too will be great, but his younger brother will be greater than he and his descendants will be numerous among the nations. He blessed them that day and said, Israel will bless by you, saying, May God make you like Ephraim and Menashe—and he put Ephraim before Menashe. (48:8–20)

The subordinate position of the elder Menashe had already been hinted at at the time of his birth and naming by Joseph:

> Joseph called the name of the firstborn MêNaŠe, for God has made me forget [NaŠaNi] all my trouble and all my father's house. (41:51)

NaŠaNi appears to be a verbal play on the word meaning "second," ŠeNi[8]—just as there was in the birth of the sons of Tamar (38:28–29), where ŠaNi, "the red thread," was a play on ŠeNi, "second." The naming of Menashe may also have reference to Jacob's wrestling with his adversary in Genesis 32, where Jacob's wounding in his thigh-joint at the place of the tendon called GiD HaNaŠe portends the rivalry among his progeny.

Jacob's blessing of his grandsons plays off the blessing by his own father Isaac of his sons in Genesis 27. Jacob, here called Israel, is blind like his father before him, and wishes to bestow his blessing before he dies. Despite his blindness, he accomplishes what he set out to do in spite of Joseph's attempted correction. Isaac's blindness was the real thing—he was deceived by his younger son, with the aid of Rebecca, into thinking that Jacob was actually the older Esau. Isaac's gropings were those of a blind old man, confused by the incongruity of the voice of Jacob issuing from a body with the hairy arms and hunter's clothing that properly belonged to Esau. The patriarchal Jacob/Israel, by contrast, is the one who controls the situation when he bestows his blessing. Note the ironical juxtaposition at the beginning of the passage: "Israel saw the sons of Joseph . . . Israel's eyes were dim with age, he could not see . . . ." Israel is blind, but his blindness does not prevent him from seeing in a way that Isaac could not. Israel, like his father, transposes the blessings of the older and the younger—but he does it knowingly—while the two boys whose blessings he thus switches are unaware of what is happening above their heads. This is Jacob's final self-justification: The younger *will* be greater. In the last of the series of deceptive encounters between fathers and children in the book, the father finally turns the tables on his offspring.

Relationships of kinship are presented as polarizations of proximity and distance. Closeness is the occasion for deception, the familiar cloaks the hidden, the known occludes the unknown. The quintessential expression of the deceptiveness of intimacy is conveyed, as we saw in an earlier chapter, in the sexual knowledge that at the same time binds and separates men and women. It is not only ignorance that deceives, but knowledge too—the familiarity that forestalls questioning.

In the very first relationship between two human beings, that between Eve and Adam, a kinship which began in the literal identity of shared flesh is finally severed completely by the introduction of clothing at the end of the Tree of Knowledge story. Clothing and symbols both subserve the function of conveying meaning at the same time as they conceal it. And many of the instances of knowledge are ambiguous and expressed with irony; Lot only "knows" his daughters when he is unaware of what he and they are doing, Judah only "knows" Tamar because he is ignorant of who she is. And one might argue further, that some of the instances of ignorance have elements of ambivalence, or even disingenuousness—the line between ignorance and ignoring is not clear. Do Noah and Lot really have no idea who their children are? Are Jacob and Judah really completely unaware of how their actions affect their fathers, and their sons?

The disparity between the hidden essential and the externally visible is carried over into the understanding of events by the protagonists also, as we have seen. The veil that obscures the true nature of reality becomes more and more impenetrable as we progress through the Book of Genesis. But the universes that coexist on the two sides of the veil are none other than the two worlds which we found delineated in the two Creation accounts at the very beginning of Genesis—the worlds determined by the different perspectives of God and humans. The two perspectives are separated into two parallel accounts of the world in the Creation itself. As we saw in Chapter 2, the first account is God's, and thus not comprehensible; the second is man's, rooted in his own needs and desires. The two realities continue to course alongside one another throughout the book, as the relationship between them becomes at the same time both more and less evident. As we saw when we examined communication between God and humans, the connection between the two spheres becomes progressively more tenuous. On the other hand, if we look at the unfolding of the story of Joseph and his brothers at the end of the book, we see that the two perspectives—which start out as distinct from one another at the beginning of the story—are completely integrated by the time we get to the end. What had begun as two irreconcilable ways of seeing at the beginning of Genesis are finally seen to describe a single reality. And the bridge between the two worlds is the knowledge that so often eludes the actors in the drama.

Notes

1. The prelude to the meeting of Joseph with his brothers (who then throw him into a pit) may include a preparatory encounter with a mysterious stranger—like the meeting of Jacob with "the man" that we discussed in Chapter 6. Jacob, characteristically blind to the explosive situation for which he is largely responsible, sends Joseph out by himself to visit his brothers who are pasturing in Shechem. The situation in which Joseph finds himself is similar to that of Jacob when he approached Esau: The guilty younger brother, who has been favored by his father over his older brother(s) (unwittingly, in the case of Isaac and Jacob), sets out to meet the wronged elder brother, or, in this case, brothers. As in Jacob's case, the guilty brother is met on the way by a stranger, a "man."

> Israel said to Joseph, Your brothers are pasturing in Shechem, let me send you to them; and he said, I am ready. He said to him, Go and see how your brothers are faring and how the flocks are faring, and let me know. He sent him from the Hebron valley and he came to Shechem. A man found him wandering about in the field and asked him, What are you looking for? He said, I am looking for my brothers; can you tell me where they are pasturing? The man said, They have left here, for I heard them say, Let us go to Dothan. So Joseph went after his brothers and found them in Dothan. They saw him from afar, and before he could get near them they conspired to kill him. (37:13–18)

Joseph's search for his brothers, besides its symbolic overtones, is the occasion for the appearance of a "man" who directs him to their new whereabouts. Joseph's perilous situation as he seeks his brothers, alone and far from home, seems to call for a prophylactic prior meeting and struggle with a stranger in order that the actual confrontation with his brothers can take place without danger—as happened with Jacob before meeting Esau, and Moses before meeting Pharaoh. However, at Joseph's meeting with the stranger, *nothing* happens; the veiled warning that the man conveys to Joseph—"Your brothers are not where you think they are"—has no consequences. The imminent peril of the fraternal confrontation is not exorcised in a preparatory struggle, and the actual meeting ends in disaster. In a way, Joseph's encounter thus fits into the paradigm of the mysterious pre-meeting that portends the outcome of the following confrontation. In keeping with the tenor of the story of Joseph, however, the meeting with the man brings with it no enlightenment or strengthening for Joseph, and no illumination of the prevailing darkness. The light will break through only later, after the brothers have been subjected to both tribulation and mystification.

2. Why Simeon? The story is very precise on this point. Joseph's imprisonment of Simeon is told in the following context:

> Reuben responded to them and said, Didn't I tell you not to sin with the boy, but you did not listen ... And they did not know that Joseph understood because there was an interpreter between them ... He took Simeon from them and imprisoned him right before their eyes. (42:22–24)

He would have taken Reuben, the eldest and therefore most responsible, but after hearing what Reuben had to say he was forced to take Simeon, the second eldest.

3. David Sykes alerted me to the word play between VaYiTNaKLu ("conspired") and VaYiTNaKeR ("behaved as a stranger").

4. The text displays in a subtle way the movement of Joseph's relationship with his brothers in terms of the eventual replacement of the absence of "peace" by its final attainment, however reluctant. Thus, at the beginning of the story (37:2–4) we have Joseph's brothers unable to speak to him in a civil manner—they cannot speak to him "with peace" or *shalom*:

> ... Joseph at seventeen tended the flocks with his brothers, assisting the sons of Bilha and the sons of Zilpa his father's wives, and Joseph brought bad reports about them to their father. Israel loved Joseph the best of all his sons because he was a son of his old age, and he made him a special coat. His brothers saw that their father loved him the best of all his brothers, and they hated him and could not speak to him without rancor [LêŠaLoM, lit. "with peace" or "in peace"].

There follows here the account of Joseph's dreams and the reactions of his brothers and his father. The text continues:

> His brothers went to pasture their father's flocks in Shechem. Israel said to Joseph, Your brothers are pasturing in Shechem, let me send you to them; and he said, I am ready [HiNeNi, lit. "Here I am"]. He said to him, Go and see how your brothers are faring [ŠêLoM AHeKa, lit. "the peace of your brothers"] and how the flocks are faring [ŠêLoM HaŞoN], and let me know. He sent him from the Hebron valley and he came to Shechem. A man found him

wandering about in the field and asked him, What are you looking
for? He said, I am looking for my brothers; can you tell me where
they are pasturing? The man said, They have left here, for I heard
them say, Let us go to Dothan. So Joseph went after his brothers
and found them in Dothan. They saw him from afar, and before he
could get near them they conspired to kill him. (37:12–18)

I have translated this much of the relevant passages in order to suggest
that Joseph's mission to his brothers did not lack its share of ambivalence.
Jacob sends him to see about the welfare of the brothers and the flocks using
the Hebrew word for "peace"—*shalom* (ŠaLoM)—which is also the word
that described how the brothers could not speak to Joseph.

Further, Jacob's asking that Joseph return a report of his brothers recalls
exactly what he had been doing earlier, an activity that surely contributed
to his brothers' hatred.

There is some play with the same word—ŠaLoM—in two exchanges with
the unsuspecting brothers much later on (Genesis 43). One of the functions
of the word in that context is to force the brothers to speak of *shalom* to
Joseph—that is, they are forced to respond to him with the "shalom" that
they could not bring themselves to give him earlier. Thus, when the brothers tell Joseph's steward that they have brought back with them the money
that they had found miraculously returned to them in their sacks, he reas-
sures them:

> Peace [ŠaLoM] to you [that is, "Everything is all right with you"],
> do not fear; your God and the God of your fathers has given you a
> hidden gift in your sacks—I received your money . . . . (43:23)

And then, once they have been brought into Joseph's house and have given
him their gift and bowed down to the ground before him:

> [Joseph] asked about their welfare [LêŠaLoM], and he said, Is it
> well [HaŠaLoM] with your old father of whom you have spoken;
> is he still alive? And they said, Your servant our father is well
> [ŠaLoM], he is still alive; and they bowed and prostrated them-
> selves. (43:27–28)

Joseph inquires about the *shalom* of his brothers—as his father had bidden
him to do long ago—and in addition asks his brothers about the *shalom*
of his father. In response, the brothers are constrained to say "shalom" to
Joseph, thus unknowingly reversing their earlier refusal to speak *shalom* to
him. The response of the brothers in the original Hebrew makes this con-

nection clearer, because their answer begins with the word "shalom"; they actually answer Joseph's question by saying "Shalom . . . ."

Joseph offers his brothers peace at the beginning of the passage, and peace will soon be brought into the turbulent fraternal relationship.

5. In the story of Jacob and Laban also, Laban's going to shear his sheep is the occasion for Jacob's stealing away with his wives and flocks and for Rachel's theft of her father's household gods (31:19). Even more interesting is the account in II Samuel 13 of the premeditated deceitful murder of Amnon by his half-brother Absalom at the sheep-shearing. Amnon, one of the sons of David (the descendant of Peretz, son of Judah and Tamar), rapes his half-sister, also called Tamar. The crime is then avenged by her full brother Absalom. We have in this story several of the elements of the Joseph story, including an incorporation of the apparently parenthetical Judah and Tamar episode. In the story in II Samuel there appear competition and crime among siblings, an incestuous union between a brother and a sister (perhaps a dark play on a levirate marriage), and the suffering by David of the consequences of discord among his children—for in addition to the death of Amnon, David also loses Absalom later on. Tamar in II Samuel is described as wearing the same kind of "ornamented coat" (KêToNeT PaSiM, "coat of many colors") that Joseph wears. After Amnon rapes her and has her thrown out of his chamber, we read:

> She was wearing an ornamented coat, because thus were the virgin daughters of the king cloaked, and his servant put her outside and locked the door after her. Tamar put dust on her head and rent the ornamented coat that she wore, and she put her hand on her head and went about wailing. (13:18–19)

The episodes in Genesis and in II Samuel are the only places in the Bible where this expression for a special coat is found. Joseph's wearing of this royal garment portends his rise to eminence in Egypt.

6. The story of Judah and Tamar has a number of other connections with the story of David. Judah goes to his friend, an Adullamite named ḤiRa; Adullam is a place name that figures in the story of David, and David's ally is the king of Sidon, who is named ḤiRaM. Judah takes as a wife the unnamed daughter of a man named Shua. The Hebrew for "daughter of Shua," BaT Šuʻa, sounds remarkably like the name of David's wife BaT ŠeBa (Bathsheba); and in fact, David's wife is actually called BaT Šuʻa instead of BaT ŠeBa in I Chronicles 3:5 (pointed out to me by David Sykes). Tamar is associated with the death of Judah's two older sons, as the loss of David's two

sons Amnon and Absalom begins with their sister Tamar. Judah's surviving son is Shela (ŠeLa), whose name is similar both in sound and in one of its meanings ("serenity") to David's surviving son from Bathsheba, ŠêLoMo (Solomon), related to ŠaLoM, "peace." Thus, the story of Judah and Tamar is a rough sketch of a part of the history of King David and his family, over and above being the account of the birth of David's ancestor Peretz. See also the next note.

7. Some of the names of the characters in the Book of Ruth play on the names in the story of Judah and Tamar, as the story of Ruth also plays on the episode in Genesis. The Book of Ruth tells of a man from the region of Judah who leaves his people and moves to a foreign country. There, his two sons die childless. Like the sons of Judah in Genesis, their names reflect their fates: One is named MaḤLoN, from the root meaning "illness," and the other is called KiLioN, meaning "destruction." When the widowed mother of the dead brothers decides to return to her homeland, her two daughters-in-law insist on accompanying her, and she attempts to dissuade them. The daughter-in-law who turns around and goes back to Moab is named ʻoRPa, which is a play on the Hebrew expression for turning one's back—"to present the back of the neck (ʻoReP)." The second young widow, Ruth, is taken in a form of levirate marriage "to perpetuate the name of the deceased" (Ruth 4:10) by Boaz, who is a descendant of Peretz, son of Judah and Tamar. Interestingly, the institution of the levirate is expressed here—and nowhere else in the Bible—in terms of "redemption and exchange" (Ruth 4:7); the word for "exchange" is TêMuRa, which I suggested underlies the name Tamar. More explicitly related to the story of Judah is the wish expressed by the townsmen of Boaz on his marriage to Ruth: "May your house be like the house of Peretz whom Tamar bore to Judah" (Ruth 4:12).

The mother of the two sons—and mother-in-law of Ruth—is Naomi, meaning "pleasant" or "sweet," who, on her ignominious return to her homeland accompanied only by her one widowed daughter-in-law, tells the townspeople to call her instead MaRa, from the root meaning "bitter." This may be a play on another possible construction of the name Tamar—from the form TaMRuRiM, "bitterness"—or else simply on the second syllable of Tamar, meaning "bitter."

8. That NaŠaNi may be a play on ŠeNi was pointed out to me by David Sykes.

EPILOGUE

Creation After Genesis

CHAPTER 8

The Last Creation: The Sea of Reeds and Moses the Protector

THE CREATION IN GENESIS 1 IS THE MODEL FOR THE re-creation that takes place when the waters of the Flood recede and Noah with his family and the animals leave the ark and repopulate the earth. The Flood is a return to the watery void that preceded the original Creation, and the emergence of dry land from the water marks the start of the re-creation, as the appearance of the dry land constituted an early step in the first Creation. We noted other allusions to the first Creation in the Flood story: blessings of fertility, a Tree of Ignorance contrasted with a Tree of Knowledge, the drunken stupor of Noah and his removal of his clothing contrasted with the opening of the eyes of Adam and his wife that leads them to clothe themselves. There are echoes of Noah in the story of Lot and his daughters, and echoes of these echoes in the episode of Judah and Tamar, but once we leave Noah we are done with Creation accounts in the Book of Genesis. However, the reconstitution of the world after the Flood is not the last of the Creations, for we find another Creation story later on in the Pentateuch. In this chapter we go beyond our reading of Genesis in order to see how the Creation is evoked in a third Creation—the birth of the nation of Israel—as told at the beginning of the Book of Exodus.

The Book of Exodus begins the story of the bondage of the Israelites in Egypt, their liberation, and their subsequent wanderings in the wilderness—a history that is continued in the remaining books of the Pentateuch. Exodus thus marks a break with the narratives in Genesis about the beginning of the world and the adventures of the Patriarchs.[1] In this chapter, we will see allusions to the earliest narra-

THE SERPENT'S SKIN

tives of Genesis—those concerning the Creation and the Flood—in the initial portions of the Book of Exodus. Since a new beginning for the Hebrews starts to unfold in Exodus, it might not be surprising to find links with the earlier beginnings marked out in Genesis—to find that the very first events in the history of the world serve as models for later events. We will see that this kind of relationship does in fact hold between the early parts of Genesis and the early part of Exodus. Moreover, the continuation of the story of the Exodus transforms some of the motifs of the Creation by incorporating them into an overarching symbolism of gestation and birth. And finally, we will find that some of these themes—initiated in Genesis and developed in Exodus—are put to use elsewhere in the Bible, and are reflected in the rabbinic literature of the Mishna and the Talmud.

Emergence from Chaos

The Book of Exodus opens with an enumeration of the progeny of Jacob who came down to the land of Egypt, and with the death of that entire generation. Our attention is then immediately directed to the awesome fecundity of the Children of Israel in their new land:

> The Children of Israel were fruitful, and teemed, and multiplied, and were mighty [in numbers] to a great extent, and the land was filled with them. (Exodus 1:7)

Echoed here are the blessings that accompanied the two earlier beginnings in the Book of Genesis: the blessing to the first man and woman at the time of the Creation—"Be fruitful and multiply, and fill the land and rule over it" (1:28); and that to Noah and his sons at the time of the second beginning, after the great Flood—"Be fruitful and multiply and fill the land" (9:1), and "Be fruitful and multiply, teem on the land and multiply in it" (9:7).

This is the start of a broad parallel between the initial parts of Genesis and Exodus, for just as Genesis treats the beginning of the history of man as a species (Adam and Eve)—and as individual, chosen members of the species (Noah, Abraham, Isaac, Jacob, Joseph)—so Exodus deals with the beginnings of the history of a nation, the nation of Israel.

In the popular Hebrew nomenclature, the Book of Exodus is known as *Shemot*, the Book of Names, because it begins with the sentence "These are the names of the Children of Israel who came to Egypt with Jacob, each man came with his family: Reuben, Simeon, Levi and Judah; Issachar, Zebulun . . . ." and so on through all the progeny of Jacob. The succeeding verses tell of the death of Joseph and all his generation, and of the vast proliferation of the Children of Israel in Egypt, as we saw.

After the forebears who first come into Egypt are named down to the last man, the Israelites in their numbers then become anonymous, a teeming horde that fills the land. The loss of names of the Children of Israel is seen at the beginning of the story of Moses, when Moses, his father, mother, and sister is each mentioned, but not by name:

> A man of the house of Levi went and married a daughter of Levi. The woman conceived and bore a son, and she saw that he was beautiful, and she hid him for three months. She could no longer hide him, so she took for him a basket of wicker and daubed it with bitumen and pitch and put the child in it, and she put it among the reeds at the edge of the Nile. His sister stood some distance away to see what would happen to him. (2:1–4)

The only name that appears is Levi, just listed among the sons of Jacob who went down with him to Egypt. Why is there no naming of Moses and his family—especially in view of the detailed listing of the names of the original immigrants to Egypt just a few verses earlier?

Naming in Genesis is one of the acts that God—and then the first man—performs at the Creation in order to further define the various components of the world. The loss of the names of the Israelites in Egypt is a sign of a return to chaos, to the undifferentiated state that precedes Creation. The Israelite masses merit names only in Exodus 6, just as God is about to initiate their deliverance by smiting the Egyptians with His ten plagues:

> These are the chiefs of their clans: The sons of Reuben the firstborn of Israel are Chanoch and Palu, Chetzron and Karmi, these are the families of Reuben. The sons of Simeon are Yemuel and Yamin and Ohad and Yachin and Tzochar and Saul the son of the Canaanite woman, these are the families of Simeon . . . . (6:14–25)

189

The list ends with the tribe of Levi, where the parents of Moses and his brother Aaron are finally named. The naming of the Israelites marks the beginning of their emergence from the undifferentiated chaos of slavery.

Separation and Splitting

The major work of creation at the beginning of Genesis was accomplished by separation—of light from darkness, heaven from earth, water from dry land. Similarly, in Exodus the Israelites are separated from the Egyptians, as is repeatedly stated in the story of the plagues:

> On that day I will set apart the land of Goshen where My people are, so that the wild beasts will not be there . . . And I will make a distinction between My people and your people . . . . (8:18–19)
> The Lord will set apart the cattle of Israel from the cattle of Egypt, and none of those of the Children of Israel will die. (9:4)
> The hail struck everything in the field in Egypt, from man to beast, and the hail struck all the grass of the field, and broke all the trees of the field. Only in the land of Goshen where the Children of Israel were was there no hail. (9:25–26)
> Moses stretched out his hand to the sky and there was thick darkness in all the land of Egypt for three days . . . but for all the Children of Israel there was light in their dwelling places. (10:22–23)
> Every firstborn in the land of Egypt will die, from the firstborn of Pharaoh sitting on his throne to the firstborn of the maidservant behind the millstone, and the firstborn of all the cattle . . . but for all the Children of Israel not a dog will bark [lit. "whet its tongue"] at man or beast, so that you may know that the Lord is setting apart Egypt from Israel. (11:5–7)

And in Exodus 12 God smites the Egyptian firstborn, but "passes over" the houses of the Israelites, thus inaugurating the first Passover.

The seminal separations that resulted in the seas, land, and heavens of today were executed by God on the second and third days of the Creation, after the creation of light and separation of light from darkness on the first day:

> God said, Let there be an expanse in the midst of the water and let it separate between water and water. God made the expanse, and it separated between the water that was above the expanse and the water that was

below the expanse, and it was so. God called the expanse Sky, and it was evening and it was morning, a second day.

God said, Let the waters below the sky gather into one place and let the dry land appear, and it was so. God called the dry land Land and the gathering of waters He called Seas, and God saw that it was good. (Genesis 1:6–10)

These particular separations are recalled in the final severing of the connection between the Israelites and their Egyptian oppressors, a separation that results in the emergence of the Children of Israel as an independent and unified nation. Three days after the Israelite exodus from Egypt, Pharaoh and his army set out in pursuit of the Hebrews with the aim of returning them to Egypt and to their bondage. The Egyptian forces approach the Children of Israel at the edge of the Sea of Reeds, where, at God's command:

Moses stretched his arm out over the sea, and the Lord drove the sea with a strong east wind all night; He turned the sea into dry ground and the waters split. The Children of Israel entered into the middle of the sea on dry land, and the water formed a wall for them on their right and on their left. (Exodus 14:21–22)

The splitting of water from water and the emergence of dry land from the water are echoes of the Creation. Where the account in Genesis tells of the beginnings of the world, the stories of Exodus depict the beginnings of the nation of Israel as a creation that is similarly accomplished by separation—not only of the Children of Israel from the Egyptians, but even by the same kind of manipulations of water and earth that were executed by God at the very first beginning.

The Egyptian armies follow the Children of Israel into the sea, but once the Israelites have safely crossed over, God commands Moses to stretch his arm out over the sea once again and the waters come crashing down on the Egyptians. The separated waters come together once more, as had happened in the time of Noah. The drowning of the Egyptians in the sea is certainly retribution for their casting the Hebrew children into the Nile, and imparts an additional meaning to the sign of the waters of the Nile turning to blood (4:9 and 7:17–21). Blood taking the place of water in the Nile refers to the

Hebrew children drowned in the Nile, but also to the future death by drowning of the Egyptians.

The splitting of the sea and the appearance of dry land on which the Israelites were able to cross allude to the separation of the waters and the appearance of land in the Creation. The splitting of the Sea of Reeds is in turn alluded to in the story of the entry of the Israelites into the Promised Land under the leadership of Moses' successor, Joshua the son of Nun. We read in the Book of Joshua that when the Israelites stand on the bank of the River Jordan, prepared to leave the wilderness and enter the Promised Land, the river's flow is arrested:

> As those carrying the Ark [ARoN, not the same as the word used for the ark of Noah, which is TeBa] came up to the Jordan and the feet of the priests carrying the Ark dipped into the edge of the water—the Jordan was full up to all its banks all the time of the harvest—the waters descending from above stood still, piled up as a single heap . . . The priests carrying the Ark of the Lord's Covenant stood on dry ground in the middle of the Jordan, and all Israel crossed on dry ground until the whole nation finished crossing the Jordan. (Joshua 3:15–17)

The description of the waters piled up as a heap repeats the description of the waters standing "as a heap" at the crossing of the Sea of Reeds (Exodus 15:8). And Joshua himself makes sure that the Israelites make the connection to the crossing of the sea in the days of Moses:

> You shall tell your children that on dry ground did Israel cross this Jordan; that the Lord your God dried up the waters of the Jordan before you until you crossed, just as the Lord your God did to the Sea of Reeds, which He dried up before us until we crossed. (Joshua 4:22–23)

This is one of several instances where Joshua imitates the actions of his mentor Moses, all with the purpose of demonstrating to the people that God supports Joshua just as God supported Moses, and that Joshua is therefore entitled to the people's confidence. Thus:

> On that day the Lord exalted Joshua in the eyes of all Israel, and they revered him as they revered Moses all the days of his life. (Joshua 4:14)

The Long Gestation

The image of the Children of Israel crossing through the water on dry land, in addition to its connection with the splitting of the waters and the appearance of dry land in the Creation, also serves as a metaphor for birth. This is most clearly suggested in the description of the Israelites' crossing of the sea after the Exodus. The fearful ex-slaves hesitate at the sea's edge, the waters part, they cross, they emerge on the other shore, and the waters close up behind them. This image of birth is presented in the context of images of maturation and development that refer to the biological process of human gestation, as we will see.

The first mention of the exile into Egypt occurs in one of God's appearances to Abram (before his name was changed to Abraham), in Genesis 15:12–14:

> The sun was near setting and a deep sleep overcame Abram, a great dark fear came over him. He said to Abram, Know that your offspring will be sojourners in a land not their own, and they will enslave them and torment them for four hundred years. And I will also execute judgment upon the nation whom they serve, and afterward they will depart with great wealth.

In the account of the Exodus itself, the time spent by the Children of Israel in Egypt is given as 430 years (Exodus 12:40–41), perhaps implying that the period of enslavement and affliction began only thirty years after they entered Egypt.[2] In any case, the bondage recounted in the Book of Exodus is the fulfillment of the prophecy to Abraham. After the four hundred years in Egypt, the people spend the next forty years wandering in the wilderness, until they reach the Jordan (Numbers 14:33–34; 32:13; 33:38; and elsewhere). The forty years of wandering in the wilderness had been ordained by God so that all the members of a sinful generation would die out before their offspring would be permitted to enter the Promised Land (Numbers 14:33). Forty years is a time period representing a generation, and four hundred years is thus not an arbitrary period of time signifying a long duration, but is rather an intensive multiple of forty years.

The basic association of a period of time based on the number forty may be with the forty weeks of gestation, and secondarily also with the idea that the fetus attains its form in the first forty days of gestation, as asserted in the Babylonian Talmud (*Nida* 30a).[3] This idea may be based in a theory of embryology according to which the forty weeks of gestation were divided into seven periods of forty days each, corresponding to the seven days of Creation. A statement elsewhere in the Babylonian Talmud supports this idea: Up until the fortieth day of embryonic development the fetus is considered to be without form, like "mere water" (*Yevamot* 69b), and thus like the world before God began his work of Creation.

Seen from this perspective, four hundred years in Egypt is to the Children of Israel as forty weeks in the womb is to the fetus. Perhaps the parallel between the sojourn in Egypt and gestation in the womb is also hinted at in the Hebrew term for Egypt, MiSRaYiM, which can be construed as deriving from MeSaR, a narrow, constrained space — for example, in the Book of Psalms: "From distress (HaMeSaR, lit. "the narrow strait") I called out to God; God answered me in the broad open space" (Psalms 118:5). After four hundred years in the confining womb of Egypt, the Children of Israel are born by emerging from the waters of the Sea of Reeds.

The paradigm of a collective gestation followed by birth is repeated in the Israelites' forty years of wandering in the wilderness and their subsequent crossing of the waters of the Jordan on dry land in the time of Joshua. The crossing of the Sea of Reeds signified the creation of the people of Israel by its extraction from the bondage of Egypt; the crossing of the Jordan marks the transformation of the Israelites from a nomadic band wandering in the wilderness into a proper nation living in a homeland. Both cases of the Hebrews' crossing the water on dry land to emerge transformed on the other shore are preceded by a gestation, as indicated by a preceding period of forty or four hundred years.

During the four hundred years in Egypt the people grow from a collection of seventy individuals (Exodus 1:5) into a nation numbering six hundred thousand (12:37). In the forty years of wandering in the wilderness, the Israelites undergo a second transformation. From a nation of slaves newly escaped from bondage in a foreign land they become a nation of masters in a land of their own. The reason for the sentence of forty years of wandering is described in the story of the spies sent to scout out the Promised Land in the Book of Numbers. The spies return from their mission (of forty days) and plant fear in the people's hearts with their description of the terrible might of the nations whom they must defeat in order to win the land. The people's response betrays their weakness:

> The whole congregation raised their voices and the people wept on that night. All the Children of Israel cried to Moses and Aaron, all the congregation said to them, Would that we had died in the land of Egypt or that we had died in this wilderness; why does the Lord bring us to this land to die by the sword, and our women and children to go into captivity—it would be better for us to return to Egypt. And they said to one another, Let us appoint a leader and return to Egypt. (Numbers 14:1–4)

God then tells Moses and Aaron that this generation of the Children of Israel, those born in Egypt, will not enter the Promised Land but will wander in the wilderness for forty years until they all die out. During those forty years the children of that generation will grow up to take the place of their elders, and they, the children, will be the ones to take possession of the land of their ancestors. The forty-year wait thus serves two purposes—it allows for the old generation to disappear and for the new generation to mature.

A similar supplanting of one generation by another had taken place with the destruction by the Flood of all the land-creatures, followed by the repopulation of the world by Noah and those rescued by him in the ark, as recounted in the Book of Genesis and discussed in Chapter 4. And the rain falls for forty days and forty nights:

> For in seven more days I will cause it to rain on the land for forty days and forty nights and I will wipe out all the living things that I have made from the face of the earth. (7:4)
> The rain was on the land for forty days and forty nights. (7:12)
> The Flood was on the land for forty days and the waters increased and lifted the ark and it rose from the land. (7:17)

The world reverts to the state of formlessness that prevailed before the Creation, but at the same time the stage is being set for the second Creation that will begin with Noah and the living creatures that leave the ark with him. The dry land emerges from the waters of the Flood and Noah's family and the animals fill the earth once again. Periods of forty years or four hundred years or forty days are periods of chaos during which prior worlds are destroyed, but at the same time, these are periods of formation and preparation for the appearance of a new reality.

Water and Rebirth

The motif of emerging from water as a new birth is encapsulated in the rite of immersion mandated by Jewish law for an individual who makes the transition from the ritually impure to the ritually pure state. Washing in water is prescribed as a part of the purification procedure for a number of types of ritual impurity treated in the Books of Leviticus and Numbers involving, among others, contact with the dead or recovery from certain diseases. This washing was determined by the rabbis to mean immersion of the whole body in water (BT *Eruvin* 4b). The impure person emerges from the water purified. A similar immersion is prescribed for someone who undergoes conversion to Judaism, another kind of rebirth.

The rabbinic literature concerning ritual immersion suggests a coalescence of themes from the early parts of both Genesis and Exodus. Ritual purification and conversion are symbolic rites of rebirth for which emerging from water is a concrete expression. This immersion takes place in a bath called a *mikve*—literally, a "gathering (of waters)." This word appears for the first time in the Creation account in Genesis 1, where it denotes the gathering of the lower waters into seas on the third Creation day, allowing dry land to appear.

The water of the *mikve* must come directly from a natural source— either a spring or other natural body of water, or from rainwater—and may not have been collected through human agency and then poured into the *mikve* (BT *Shabbat* 15a and elsewhere). Thus, as in the Creation and in the Flood, the two waters, the upper and the lower, are invoked. Immersion as part of the purification rite takes place after a seven-day preparatory period—perhaps echoing the seven Creation days—just as other biblical transitions are often accomplished in a seven-day period.

In addition to its function as a metaphor for the gestation preceding birth, ritual immersion also refers in an indirect way to the duration of gestation. Despite the absence of a forty-day gestation period in the passage from the impure to the pure state, or in the transformation from Gentile to Jew, the number is not completely passed over.[4] According to rabbinic law (BT *Mikvaot* 1:7; *Eruvin* 4b), the *mikve* must contain at least forty *se'ah* of water,[5] which is considered to be the minimum volume that will completely envelop the human body. Both the laws of the *mikve* and the statement that the human embryo is like water during the first forty days of gestation (see above) suggest that the rabbis were cognizant of the connections among these three concepts—the number, the element, and the ontogenetic process—and incorporated them into ritual practice.

Emergence from water represents the attainment of form after a state of formlessness, like emergence from the womb and like the earliest stages of embryonic development in the womb. The association of these processes with the number forty is most simply explained by the forty weeks of gestation, as we discussed above. However, there is another possible association between water and the number forty that comes from a completely different direction.

In Hebrew, as in Greek, letters were used to represent numbers,[6] so that the numbers one through ten were represented by *alef* through *yod*, multiples of ten by *kaf* through *ṣade*, and multiples of one hundred (up to four hundred) by *qof* through *tav*. The letter used for forty is called *mem*, the root meaning "water," and the early form of this letter was correspondingly a wavy line that represented water. Thus, *mem* means both "water" and "forty."

It may be that water and the number forty were associated because both are connected with gestation, or that the fortuitous association of the number with the element by way of the alphabet was noted and exploited early on. In any case, it would be interesting to see whether other numbers might not also reflect their associations with particular concepts in the assignment of numerical values to letters.

Moses and Noah

We suggested above that the drowning of the Egyptians in the Sea of Reeds and the dying off of the first generation of liberated Israelites during the forty years in the wilderness carry associations with the flood of Noah. But the introduction to the Book of Exodus also reveals a more explicit reference to the story of Noah and the Flood:

> Then Pharaoh commanded all his people and said, Every boy that is born throw into the Nile, but let every girl live.
> A man of the house of Levi went and married a daughter of Levi. The woman conceived and bore a son, and she saw that he was beautiful, and she hid him for three months. She could no longer hide him, so she took for him a basket of wicker and daubed it with bitumen and pitch and put the child in it, and she put it among the reeds at the edge of the Nile. His sister stood at a distance to see what would happen to him. (1:22–2:4)

We see here a parallel to the continuation of the history of humanity in Genesis, in the story of the destruction of all the inhabitants of the earth by the waters of the Flood. In Genesis, all the land-creatures die, with the exception of Noah and those who find safety with him in an ark waterproofed with pitch; likewise in Exodus, while the other children are drowned in the Nile, Moses is saved in a basket rendered waterproof with bitumen and pitch. The same word, TeBa, is used for the basket of Moses and for the ark of Noah. The word TeBa appears only in these two contexts, and nowhere else, in the Bible. The fact that the basket holding the baby Moses could have been called ARoN, "casket," or SaL, "basket," while Noah's craft could have been called ONiYa or SêPiNa, "ship" or "boat," reinforces the suggestion that the two arks should be seen as analogous.

Moses appears as a Noah in the subsequent story of the peregrinations of the Israelites in the wilderness as told in the Books of Exodus and Numbers. He is almost forced to play the role of a Noah in relation to the wayward Children of Israel at several junctures—but he refuses to let himself be saved while his people are destroyed. For example, after the Israelites sin by worshipping the Golden Calf, God says to Moses:

> Now let Me be, My wrath will blaze at them and I will destroy them, and I will make you into a great nation. Moses pleaded with the Lord his God and said, Why, Lord, should Your wrath blaze against Your people whom You took out of the land of Egypt with great might and with a powerful hand . . . And the Lord relented of the evil that He had intended to do to His people. (Exodus 32:10–14)

Similarly, after the spies return from the land of Canaan and incite the Israelites to repudiate the land promised them by God, God threatens to destroy the people and begin again with Moses—and once again Moses prevails upon God to forgive His people (Numbers 14:11–20). Moses transcends Noah by refusing to be a Noah.

Women, Life, and Mother Moses

Consonant with the reigning metaphors and images of gestation, birth, and childhood that inform the first portion of the Book of Exodus are complementary motifs of maternity and of women as saviors, which may also have reference to themes first treated in Genesis. At the same time, Moses' role as protector of the Children of Israel can be seen to grow out of his own history of salvation by women.

We read at the end of the Garden of Eden story of the different roles and fates ordained by God for women and for men. Adam is condemned to earn his livelihood by toiling in suffering—by the sweat of his brow—and Eve to suffer in childbirth. This decree is fulfilled to an extreme degree at the beginning of the Book of Exodus, where we find the male Israelites toiling as slaves, and the fruit of the women's travails—their babies—destined to be killed at birth or to be thrown into the Nile. The men toil in sorrow; the women give birth in sorrow:

> The Egyptians worked the Children of Israel with back-breaking rigor. They made their lives bitter with hard work, with mortar and bricks and with all manner of work in the field, with all their back-breaking work for which they used them.
>
> The king of Egypt spoke to the midwives of the Hebrews, one of whom was named Shifra and the other Pua, and he said, When you assist the Hebrew women at their giving birth, look on the birthing-stone—if it is a boy, kill him, and if it is a girl she shall live [VêHaYa]. But the midwives feared God and they did not do as the king of Egypt told them, and they caused the boy babies to live [VaTêHaYeNa].
>
> The king of Egypt summoned the midwives and said to them, Why have you done this thing, and caused the boy babies to live [VaTêHaYeNa]? The midwives said to Pharaoh, Because the Hebrew women are not like Egyptian women, for they are robust [HaYoT, lit. "lively"], and even before the midwife comes to them they have already given birth.

> God was good to the midwives, and the people multiplied and waxed greatly. And because the midwives feared God, He established houses for them. Then Pharaoh commanded all his people and said, Throw every boy that is born into the Nile, but let every girl live [TêḤaYuN]. (1:13–22)

I have transliterated all the appearances of words built on the Hebrew root ḤYH, referring to life—five in all.[7] All of them are associated with females: with the infant girls who are to remain alive, with the midwives who cause all the babies to live, with the Hebrew women who excel in their life-giving qualities. The characterization of women as bearers of life is another link connecting the beginning of the Book of Exodus with the Creation in the Book of Genesis, where the assignment to the man and the woman of their respective modes of suffering is followed by a new definition of the role of woman as the giver of life. As we noted in our discussion of the Garden of Eden, the first account of the creation of the woman in Genesis 2 allots to the woman the role of companion and helper for the man, for "it is not good that the man is alone." Only after eating the fruit of the Tree of Knowledge is the role of the woman as the bearer of life acknowledged, when the man gives the woman the name Eve, ḤaVa, "for she is the mother of all living beings (ḤaY)"—from the same root, ḤYH.

Women as preservers of life play a major role at the beginning of Exodus. The actions of the women serve in a sense to reverse the parts played by the two genders in the Garden, where the woman was responsible for the man's disobedience to God's command. In the Book of Exodus it is men who are responsible for the death of the children, while the women do their best to frustrate the men's evil designs.

In the instruction of Pharaoh to the midwives—"if it is a boy, kill him, and if it is a girl, she shall live"—the juxtaposition of males with death and of females with life is emblematic of the opposition between the sexes at the beginning of Exodus. The primary opposition, as we will see, is not between Egyptian and Hebrew or between master and slave, but rather between men and women. On one side we have Pharaoh and the Egyptian taskmasters who torment the Israelites and threaten to kill the babies. Opposed to them stand the midwives, who refuse to carry out the king's order; the mother and sister of Moses, who hide him and watch over him as he floats in his basket on the Nile; and the daughter of Pharaoh and her maids, who rescue the boy (2:5–10). And this opposition is expressed in a rather precise manner in the various relationships among the protagonists. Thus, Pharaoh and his slave drivers oppress the Israelites, while the daughter of Pharaoh and her maidservants act in defiance of his orders and rescue the Israelite infant Moses from the Nile; the opposition between Pharaoh and his disobedient daughter contrasts with the unity of purpose of the mother of Moses and *her* daughter (there is no mention of Moses' father); the two daughters and the mother conspire to thwart the king; the sister of Moses, who watches over him from afar, contrasts with the Hebrew men, called the brothers of Moses, who strike each other and betray him to Pharaoh in the matter of Moses' slaying of the Egyptian taskmaster:

> In those days Moses grew up and went out to his brothers and saw their toils, and he saw an Egyptian man striking a Hebrew man of his brothers. He turned this way and that and saw that there was no one about, and he killed the Egyptian and hid him in the sand. He went out the next day and there were two Hebrew men fighting, and he said to the villain, Why do you strike your fellow? He answered, Who made you a lord and judge over us? Do you intend to kill me as you killed the Egyptian? Moses became afraid, and thought, So the thing is known. Pharaoh heard this and sought to kill Moses, so Moses fled from Pharaoh and dwelt in the land of Midian . . . . (2:11–15)

The opposition between men and women is in evidence even beyond the borders of the land of Egypt. After Moses arrives at a well in the land of Midian, we read:

> The priest of Midian had seven daughters, and they came and drew water and filled the troughs to water their father's flock. The shepherds came and drove them away, but Moses rose up and rescued them and watered their flock. (2:16–17)

The men seem to be at war with everyone, while the women seek only to promote and preserve life.

The sisterhood of the Hebrew women with the Egyptian women is further suggested in God's words to Moses, foretelling the future events:

> I will make the people find favor in the eyes of Egypt, and when you go
> you will not go empty-handed. Each woman will request from her female
> neighbor and from the woman who lives in her house gold utensils and
> silver utensils and clothes, and you will place them on your sons and on
> your daughters, and you will despoil Egypt. (3:21–22)

Favor is found by women in the eyes of other women, and the ben-
eficiaries are the Israelite children; the women are allies, even the
Egyptian and the Israelite women. The sole male who attempts to
bridge between the two gender roles is Moses, who takes on himself
the task of succoring those in distress. And in fulfilling this role he
comes into conflict with other men—Egyptian, Hebrew, and Midi-
anite.

The women remain outside the deadly frame of reference set up
by the men, and follow their own, separate agenda. The roles taken
by women in Exodus are analogous in this way to those they play in
Genesis, where they tend to deflect the course of events in directions
not contemplated by the men, or to circumvent or subvert the male
designs. Moreover, as in Genesis, the purposes of the women in Exodus are unified by their acting in the service of life, and specifically for
the preservation of the children. In a particularly neat example of the
characteristic opposition between men and women at the beginning
of Exodus, we have Pharaoh using the waters of the Nile to destroy
the male children, while the women use the very same waters to save
the life of the baby Moses.

The persona of Moses is shaped by the actions of the women,
and in his role as savior of the Hebrews he takes on the task that the
women have initiated. Indeed, in one of his exchanges with God,
Moses sounds much like a mother pushed to the end of her endur-
ance by a demanding child:

> Did I conceive this nation? Did I give birth to it? That You tell me, Carry it
> in your bosom as the nurse carries the suckling child to the land that You
> promised to their fathers. From where do I have meat to give to this whole
> people, who wail to me and say, Give us meat that we may eat? I cannot
> bear this people by myself, they are too much for me. (Numbers 11:12–14)

This indeed is the role of Moses, the nurturer and protector of
an immature people. The earlier life of Moses is a preparation for

this role: Until he returns to Egypt as liberator of the Israelites, the most significant influences on his own development are women. And further, these women are his deliverers, as he is later to be the deliverer of the Israelites. The female deliverers are numerous: perhaps the midwives, who refuse to murder the newborn boys; certainly Moses' mother, who sets him afloat in a small ark; his sister Miriam, who watches over him from afar; the daughter of Pharaoh and her maidservants, who rescue him from the Nile; his sister and mother once more, who nurture him for Pharaoh's daughter. And finally, in a cryptic episode when Moses is on his way back to Egypt from Midian at God's behest to liberate the Hebrews, his wife Zipporah saves him from the destroying God:[8]

> It was on the road, at the night encampment [MaLoN, a play on the root meaning "circumcision"], the Lord met him and sought to kill him. Zipporah took a flint and cut off the foreskin of her son, and touched his legs, and said, For a bridegroom of blood are you to me; when He let him alone she said, A bridegroom of blood of circumcision [MuLoT].[9] (4:24–26)

It is women who rescue Moses from malign male figures—Pharaoh and God—just as he will later rescue the Israelites from these same threatening personae. For Moses is the protector and savior of the Hebrews not only from Pharaoh, but even from God Himself, Who repeatedly threatens to destroy His people only to be dissuaded by Moses—as we saw earlier in Moses' refusal to emulate Noah.

Similar interventions on the part of Moses that succeed in saving the people from God's wrath are recounted in several other places (for example, in Exodus 32 and in Numbers 11, 14, and 16). Moses thus acts as a mother would act to protect her children, regardless of where the threat originates.

The Two Perspectives

The cosmic themes of the beginning of Genesis are not abandoned later on, but are rather brought down from their abstractness and universality and applied to the vicissitudes of human history. This development of the motif of Creation in the Book of Exodus stands alongside the earlier movement from a Creation conceived in abstract and analytic terms to one couched in terms more attuned to the concerns of mortals; this movement occurred in the transition from the first to the second Creation account in Genesis, as we saw in Chapter 2.

Creation is thus brought down to a human plane in two different ways. In Genesis, the divine point of view that is evinced in the first Creation account is succeeded by an alternative, human point of view in the second account. The two points of view are complementary, but are nonetheless distinct and conceptually mutually exclusive. The Book of Exodus, on the other hand, uses the conceptual and symbolic framework of the first Creation account of Genesis to synthesize the two ways of looking at Creation, by depicting the direct intervention of God in human affairs in order to effect another kind of Creation. The abstract structure of cosmogony—transformed by way of metaphors of birth and maternity—thus becomes the frame of reference for the genesis of a people.

Notes

1. Although, as many have noted, an attentive reading of the stories of the Patriarchs reveals parallels to the history of their descendants in Egypt (see, for example, Brettler, 53–54).

2. The classical medieval Jewish commentators struggle to reconcile this number with the duration of the exile as calculated from the life spans of those who came down to Egypt; we will consider the four-hundred-year period with respect only to its symbolic significance.

3. A forty-day period is uniquely associated with recovery from childbirth in the Book of Leviticus. There are several ways, described in Leviticus (11–15) and Numbers (19), that a person can become ritually impure, requiring that person to undergo a purification ceremony of greater or lesser elaborateness. All of the purification procedures involve some period of waiting, either overnight or seven days, for the purification to be complete. There is one circumstance, however, that calls for a much longer waiting period than all the others: A woman after childbirth must wait forty days after the birth of a son, or double that period after the birth of a daughter, before she is permitted to enter the Sanctuary (Leviticus 12).

4. A third type of passage, from the state of sinner to penitent, is also accompanied by the number forty, in the guise of the forty lashes to which

the sinner is subject (Deuteronomy 25:2–3). This function of the number forty is consistent with the role it plays in its other contexts as a marker of the transformation, often painful, from one ontogenetic state to another.

5. A volume of 250–1,000 liters, depending on exactly how the Talmudic *se'ah* is measured. See *Encyclopedia Judaica*, 2nd ed., ed. Fred Skolnik and Michael Berenbaum (Detroit: Macmillan Reference USA in association with the Keter Pub. House, 2007), 1:261, 20:708.

6. Ibid., 15:334.

7. The repeated use of the root ḤYH was pointed out to me by David Sykes.

8. Although the "bridegroom of blood" episode remains resistant to a complete explanation, it appears to have connections to several other elements in the story of the Exodus. First of all, in the verses immediately preceding the episode, God tells Moses:

> Tell Pharaoh, Thus said the Lord, Israel is My firstborn son. I have said to you, Release My son that he may serve Me, and you have refused to release him; so I will kill your firstborn son. And it was on the road, at the night encampment . . . .

In part because of this immediately preceding passage I suggest that Zipporah's symbolic slaughter was of her firstborn son, exacting from Moses the same penalty that was to be visited on Pharaoh for the same crime: unwillingness to deliver the firstborn of God. I discussed this at greater length at the end of Chapter 6.

Zipporah's actions and their results are also suggestive. She circumcises their son, touches Moses' feet, and calls her husband a "bridegroom of blood"; God then leaves Moses without killing him. This brings to mind the Paschal ritual performed immediately prior to the Exodus, when the display of blood is instrumental in the sparing of the firstborn of the Hebrews in the face of the wholesale destruction of the firstborn of the Egyptians. Moses tells the elders to slaughter a lamb and

> Take a bundle of hyssop and dip it in the blood that is in the bowl, and touch the lintel and the two door-posts with the blood from the bowl, and let no one of you leave the door of his house until morning. The Lord will come to smite Egypt, He will see the blood on the lintel and on the two door-posts, and the Lord will skip over the door and will not allow the destroyer to enter your houses to strike. (12:22–23)

Besides the likely connection to the "bridegroom of blood" episode (the blood touched to the door-posts is also reminiscent of Zipporah's touching Moses' legs), there may also be here another birth metaphor—in this case, a metaphor for the safety of the womb before birth. The people are instructed to paint the door-posts and the lintels with blood and to emerge only after the Egyptian firstborn are all destroyed. This is an inversion of the murder of the Hebrew infants by the Egyptians; the final consummation of this retribution takes place at the Sea of Reeds.

9. There is a special connection between circumcision and eligibility to participate in the Passover sacrifice:

> The Lord said to Moses and Aaron, This is the law of the Passover sacrifice, no foreigner shall eat of it. And every servant of a man acquired with his money, first circumcise him and then he may eat of it . . . If a sojourner should dwell with you and make the Passover sacrifice to the Lord, let all his males be circumcised and then he may approach to make it and he will be like a citizen of the land; no uncircumcised man shall eat of it. (12:43–48)

This connection between the sacrifice and circumcision may also underlie the exceptional character of the penalties for failure to perform these two rites. There is a general principle in Jewish law that failure to perform a positive commandment is not punishable by "extirpation" (*karet*), but this rule is abrogated in only these two instances (see BT *Keritot* 2a).

The special link between Passover and circumcision and an evocation of the bridegroom of blood are found together in the Book of Joshua. Immediately after Joshua's reenactment of the splitting of the Sea of Reeds by stopping the flow of the waters of the Jordan, allowing the Israelites to cross on dry land, we read the following:

> The Lord spoke to Joshua and said, Take from the people twelve men, one man from each tribe, and command them, Carry from here, from the Jordan, from the place where the priests stand, twelve stones, and take them with you and set them down at the night encampment [MaLoN] where you will camp tonight . . . . (4:1–3)
> The Children of Israel did so, as Joshua commanded, and they carried twelve stones from the midst of the Jordan as the Lord said to Joshua, in the number of the tribes of the Children of Israel, and they took them with them to the night encampment [MaLoN] and set them down there. (4:8)

At that time the Lord said to Joshua, Make knives of flint [ṢuRiM] and circumcise the Children of Israel once again. So Joshua made knives of flint [ṢuRiM] and circumcised the Children of Israel on the Hill of the Foreskins. This is the reason that Joshua performed the circumcision: All the males of the people who left Egypt—all the warriors—died in the wilderness on the road when they left Egypt. All the people who left were circumcised, but all the people who were born in the wilderness, on the road, on their way out of Egypt, were not circumcised. For the Children of Israel traveled in the wilderness for forty years until the death of all the warriors of the nation who had left Egypt, who had not heeded the voice of the Lord, and the Lord had sworn not to let them see the land that the Lord had promised to their fathers to give us, a land flowing with milk and honey. He set their children in their stead; them it was that Joshua circumcised, for they were uncircumcised, for they did not circumcise them on the road. When the whole nation had done being circumcised they remained in their place until they were healed . . . The Children of Israel camped in the Gilgal, and they made the Passover sacrifice on the fourteenth day of the month in the evening on the plains of Jericho. (5:2–10)

In the introduction to this episode, God tells Joshua to prepare the people for their crossing of the Jordan by collecting stones to set up when they reach the night encampment—MaLoN—on the other side. This place, designated by the same word that appears in the "bridegroom of blood" episode as a play on the word for circumcision, is also to be the site of the mass circumcision of the people in preparation for the Paschal sacrifice that will soon follow. Furthermore, Joshua is told to ready flint knives—ṢuRiM—for the circumcision, just as Zipporah used a flint—ṢoR—for the corresponding operation that she performed on her son. And the repetition of the fact that the Children of Israel who were born "on the road" had not been circumcised—unlike those who had been born in the land of Egypt and died in the wilderness—appears likewise to be an allusion to the opening of the "bridegroom of blood" narrative: "And it was on the road, at the night encampment . . ." that Zipporah circumcised her son, who had not been born in Egypt, and where Moses, of the generation born in Egypt, almost lost his life.

207